# REFLECTIONS
# ON
# EUROPE

# REFLECTIONS ON EUROPE

Edited by
DENNIS L. BARK

Hoover Institution Press
Stanford University
Stanford, California

Hoover Institution Press Publication No. 441

First printing, 1997
03  02  01  00  99  98  97        9  8  7  6  5  4  3  2  1

Manufactured in the United States of America

The paper used in this publication meets the minimum requirements of American National Standard for Information Sciences—Permanence of Paper for Printed Library Materials, ANSI Z39.48–1984. ⊚

Library of Congress Cataloging-in-Publication Data

Reflections on Europe / edited by Dennis L. Bark
       p.     cm. — (Hoover Institution Press publication ; no. 441)
    Includes bibliographical references and index.
    Contents:  Introduction / Dennis L. Bark — The American-European relationship : reflections on half a century, 1947–1997 / Dennis L. Bark — On Russia : economics and politics, heritage and tradition / Robert Conquest — A European triangle : France, Germany, and the United Kingdom / Dominique Moïsi — On Germany, Turkey, and the United States / Ludger Kühnhardt — The uncertain future of the Atlantic Alliance / Henry S. Rowen.
    ISBN 0-8179-9492-0 (alk. paper)
    1. Europe—Politics and government—1989–   2. Post-communism—Europe.   3. Europe—Foreign relations—United States.   4. United States—Foreign relations—Europe.   I. Bark, Dennis L.   II. Series: Hoover Institution Press publication ; 441.
D2009.R437   1997
327.4073—dc21                                                      97-23825
                                                                      CIP

# CONTENTS

# PREFACE

This volume is one in a series published by the Hoover Institution Press that integrates the research of prominent experts on a variety of important contemporary public policy issues. These projects are directed by Hoover fellows who assemble teams of scholars to analyze and comment on these policy issues.

Under the auspices of the Hoover program on International Rivalries and Global Cooperation, scholars consider not only questions of war and peace but all forms of rivalry and cooperation—economic, political, religious, and cultural. Within the scope of this program, Hoover fellow Dennis L. Bark coordinated this institutional research project examining the prospects for peace and prosperity in Europe during the post–cold war era. Following an overview of the past half century in Europe by Dr. Bark, researchers in this volume examine security alliances, economic policy, intra-European relations, and American-European relations.

In addition to Dennis Bark, I would like to acknowledge Patricia Baker, executive editor of the Hoover Press, and the staff at the Hoover Press for their efforts in publishing *Reflections on Europe*.

John Raisian
Director, Hoover Institution

# INTRODUCTION

The fall of the Berlin Wall was, without doubt, the most emotional event of postwar German history. The Wall was also the most powerful symbol of the *Cold War* and of the issue at stake, namely, freedom. The true irony of that memorable Thursday night on November 9, 1989, is that the Wall was opened for the same reason that it closed East Berlin in the first place: The government in East Germany hoped that freedom, rather than dictatorship, would keep people in! Since then, almost eight years have passed, and new questions, many of them consequences of the replacement of communist dictatorship with freedom, challenge both Europe and its dependable partner of the twentieth century, the United States.

The five authors of the essays in this volume bring their expertise to bear on major issues that will affect Europe's future as well as the nature of the American-European partnership. One can argue about the relative importance of the different problems facing Europe today and whether these are all addressed by one or another of the authors contributing to this volume; for example, none of the five essays deals with the crisis in former Yugoslavia. The transformations occurring there—as important, frustrating, and upsetting as they are—are not issues that will define the substance of the American-European partnership, although ethnic conflict is a tragedy that the Atlantic alliance will unquestionably encounter in the future.

The subjects discussed in the essays that follow warrant several observations at the outset. One of them is that the issues facing America and Europe today are, in some ways, more complex than the problems presented by the *Cold War*, for if the *Cold War* was an ideological conflict, it was also a conflict that was characterized by certain elements of predictability. Although the actors of the peace movement, from the 1950s to the 1980s, contended that the world faced imminent nuclear destruction if the *Cold War* got out of control, the behavior of the two superpowers was nonetheless governed by certain clear, if unspoken, rules. Chief among them was to avoid pushing the other side to the brink of war and thus to avoid backing the other side into a corner, where a flexible military response was impossible and nuclear holocaust the only alternative.

Since the collapse of communist dictatorship in Central Europe and in the former Soviet Union, however, the predictability of the *Cold War* has been replaced by instability. The conduct of foreign policy in Europe has become, in many ways, much more dangerous. The *Cold War* ended without a shot, but war has been in progress in Yugoslavia since 1991 and in different parts of the former Soviet Union as well. In addition, as this volume goes to press, conflict has arisen in Albania and conflicts in central or southern Europe are likely to develop sooner rather than later. Relations among European states are no longer governed by the unspoken rules of the *Cold War*, and the behavior of some of Europe's states is more erratic than it was during the post–World War II period from 1949 to 1989.

At the end of the twentieth century, for example, competing

forces governing in Russia—communism, capitalism, and freedom together with Russian heritage and tradition—are combined with an admixture of military power, economic risk, and political uncertainty. What issues of national interest, national security, and national defense face the Europeans and the United States, separately and together? Does NATO have a future? If so, is it from the Atlantic to the Urals? How do Russia and the newly independent states of the former Soviet Union fit into the emerging security relationships in Europe? From where will new threats to freedom and peace come, and what will these threats be? How will future threats, and conflicts, be dealt with on the continent and by whom?

Who are the leading players in post–*Cold War* Europe? England? France? Germany? What role will each play as the European Union expands? Indeed, what is the purpose of the European Union, and what ends does its expansion serve? Will the creation of a European Monetary Union take place, as scheduled, on January 1, 1999, and how will it affect Europe's competitive position vis-à-vis the United States and the Pacific? Will a strong European economic union, with one currency and a central bank, represent an asset or a liability in the American-European relationship?

Turkey is a neglected and often misunderstood pillar of NATO. Although it has been a lighthouse for the protection of freedom on the shores of the Mediterranean since 1949, its wish to join the European Union (EU) is not welcomed by its NATO partners, most of whom belong to the EU as well. What responsibilities do Turkey's NATO allies have to integrate Turkey into the future economic and political structure of the European Union? What role in Europe's future can and should Turkey play, caught between its history with *Cold War* Europe and its much older religious and cultural history with the Middle East? How does Turkey balance its interests between East and West?

A major question, for which a clear answer has yet to be found, is how the old continent will relate to the new world—to the United States—in post–*Cold War* Europe? Where do the two continents want to go in the future, how do they want to get there, and what do they want to achieve? What kind of a future does the Atlantic alliance have, as concerns the definition and defense of national interests? Will there continue to be an Atlantic community of shared values, common purposes, and constructive rivalry in the absence of a common *Cold War* threat? What new problems does the Atlantic community face in 1997, half a century after the end of World War II?

The search for answers to these questions is likely to produce increasingly acrimonious debate on the interrelationship of domestic and foreign policy issues in Europe and in the United States as the twentieth century ends and the twenty-first begins. In turn, the questions—some raised in this introduction and others in the essays themselves—must be addressed squarely and with a balanced perspective and now! Without questions, and the debate they generate in the arena of public policy formation, the old and new worlds will have difficulty determining where they want to go and how they are going to get there, and if, to paraphrase the famous catcher of the New York Yankees, Yogi Berra, they don't know where they are going, they are likely to end up somewhere else.

The five essays in this volume address different questions in different ways from different perspectives. The essay by Dominique Moïsi, deputy director of France's Institut Francais des Relations Internationale, frames the British, French, and German triangle. Ludger Kühnhardt, a young political scientist of the University of Freiburg, focuses on the often neglected but critically important relationship of Turkey to Europe and to the United States and on Germany's role in this relationship. An American perspective on the future of the Atlantic alliance, introduced by

Henry S. Rowen, concludes that "in the twentieth century both the United States and Europe have been much better off when the United States has been engaged with European security than when it was not. There is no good reason to doubt the validity of this proposition as the twenty-first century approaches. However, this leaves open the suitability of arrangements that were made during the cold war." If that conclusion is self-evident to the readers of this introduction, it is not a view universally held by either Americans or Europeans.

Related to the latter issues is the future of Russia, a country whose political system, but never its people, had a quarrel with the West during the *Cold War.* Whether the Russian people can build democracy and free markets, and can create political institutions in which Russian voters have confidence, is an open question. It is also one of the most complicated questions of the many concerning the future of Europe. Robert Conquest, whose reputation speaks for itself, addresses the question in a way few scholars are able.

Central to the future of the Atlantic alliance and the Atlantic community is how America and Europe will define what is important in the future. Fifty years ago, in the smoking ruins of Europe, it was an Austrian, Friedrich A. Hayek, who was concerned with what he called "the principal ingredients of classical liberalism"— namely, *"those values on which European civilization was built . . . the sacredness of truth . . . the ordinary rules of moral decency . . . a common belief in the value of human freedom . . . an affirmative action towards democracy . . . [and] opposition to all forms of totalitarianism, whether it be from the Right or from the Left."*

Western Europe, indeed, was rebuilt, with those ingredients providing the foundation—values of classical liberalism to which both Americans and Europeans were committed to foster and protect. Does that commitment exist as strongly fifty years later? Freedom to choose on the continent of Europe, for the first time since the Russian Revolution, does not mean that choices will be either wise or produce positive consequences. Does the expansion of European Union and the creation of vast welfare states in the western part of Europe mean that *the values of classical liberalism* are threatened? This, too, is an open question.

One thing that is clear, after all is said and done, was defined well by Edmund Burke in his "Letters of a Regicide Peace," written in 1796. Burke drew a conclusion he applied to the relationship between France and England, but it applies equally to the future relationship between America and Europe:

> Nothing is so strong a tie of amity between nation and nation as correspondence in law, customs, manners and habits of life. They have more than the force of treaties in themselves. They are obligations written in the heart.

Dennis L. Bark
Stanford, September 1997

*Dennis L. Bark*

CHAPTER ONE

# The American-European Relationship
## *Reflections on Half a Century, 1947–1997*

*Not chaos-like together crush'd and bruis'd,*
*But, as the world, harmoniously confus'd:*
*Where order in variety we see,*
*And where, though all things differ, all agree.*
Alexander Pope,
"Windsor Forest," 1704

## Reflex and Reflection

In a little book, published in 1993 in French and in 1995 in English, former French ambassador Jean-Marie Guehenno writes that the modern world is "at the inception of the fourth empire . . . closer to Rome and to the ancient world than to Christianity . . . created on the ruins of ideology, and of that Soviet empire that once claimed to be the third Rome."[1] The image, both provocative

---

1. Jean-Marie Guehenno, *The End of the Nation State* (Minneapolis: University of Minnesota Press, 1995), p. xiii. Guehenno's reference to the fourth empire is to 2 Daniel, "in which Daniel tells Nebuchadnezzar that his kingdom of gold will

and strong, is difficult to understand out of context. His description of the modern world is based on the thesis that "1989 marks the close of an era that began not in 1945 or 1917, but that was institutionalized thanks to the French Revolution, in 1789. It brings an end to the age of the nation-states."[2] Guehenno continues with two further observations, which, although he does not make the connection, are clearly related to the breakup of the Soviet empire and to the interactive, technological world of the late 1980s and 1990s:

> Powerful economic, social, and cultural forces have disrupted the circumstances that permitted the formation of the nation-states. In a world frozen by the polarization of the cold war, the effect of these forces on political institutions was checked. This effect will now be able to make itself fully felt. Radical questions will be asked, and the givens on which we have built our institutions since the eighteenth century will suffer a decisive jolt: the disjunction between our political order and the realities of today has become too great.
>
> We believed in institutions, in the force of laws to organize and control power. We persuaded ourselves that the best way of regulating the social clock was to limit power with power, to multiply the poles of force, taking care to avoid all collusion between them. These institutional constructions accompanied the diffusion of wealth and power that characterizes the modern era. . . . Because we have known nothing else, the words *democracy, politics, liberty* define our mental horizon, but we are no longer sure that we know them in a real sense, and our attachment to them has more to do with reflex than with reflection.[3]

---

be succeeded by another kingdom, of silver, then by a third, of bronze, and a fourth, of iron mixed with clay."

2. Ibid., p. x.
3. Ibid., pp. x, xi

It was this revolution—the late Albert Wohlstetter called it "the fax revolution"—that played a major role in the emergence of freedom and in the transformation of European and American politics in 1989, two centuries after the French Revolution.

The president of the Czech Republic, Vaclav Havel, chose a different focus in mid-1966. Simply and without jargon, he stressed the value of the power of reflection in contrast to the risks of reflex:

> We should stop thinking of the present state of Europe as the sunset of its energy and recognize it instead as a time of contemplation when the work of the day ceases for a while and, as the sun goes down, the rule of thought sets in.
>
> ... Europe will only be able to bear the cross of this world, and thus follow the example of Him in whom it has believed for two thousand years, and in whose name it has committed so much evil, if it first pauses and reflects upon itself, when—in the best sense of the word—it lives up to the potential inherent in the twilight to which it owes its name.[4]

It is difficult to see the triumph of freedom over tyranny in Europe as the beginning of a new empire mixed of iron and clay. But the questions Guehenno raises, and the hope for Europe that Havel feels, will affect the future of the Atlantic community.

The new reality of the Atlantic community will also be challenged by "the clash of civilizations and the remaking of the world order," which is the title of a book published in 1996 by Harvard University professor Samuel P. Huntington. He writes of global politics in a post-1989 world:

> Spurred by modernization, global politics is being reconfigured along cultural lines. Peoples and countries with similar cultures

---

4. Vaclav Havel, "The Hope for Europe," *New York Review of Books,* June 20, 1996, pp. 38–41.

are coming together. Peoples and countries with different cultures are coming apart. Alignments defined by ideology and superpower relations are giving way to alignments defined by culture and civilization. Political boundaries increasingly are redrawn to coincide with cultural ones. . . . Cultural communities are replacing Cold War blocs and the fault lines between civilizations are becoming the central lines of conflict in global politics.[5]

If "Cold War blocs" are being replaced with "cultural communities," what does this mean for the Atlantic community? Huntington's conclusion is based on a metaphor (we will hang together or hang separately) Benjamin Franklin used to describe the challenges facing the new colonial states following the American Revolution:

In the clash of civilizations, Europe and America will hang together or hang separately. In the greater clash, the global *"real* clash," between Civilization and barbarism, the world's great civilizations, with their rich accomplishments in religion, art, literature, philosophy, science, technology, morality, and compassion, will also hang together or hang separately. In the emerging era, clashes of civilizations are the greatest threat to world peace, and an international order based on civilizations is the surest safeguard against world war.[6]

To slow down what Huntington believes may be the beginning of the decline of the West, he argues that

the United States . . . should reaffirm its identity as a Western nation by repudiating multiculturalism at home, while "adopting an Atlanticist policy of close cooperation with its European part-

5. Samuel P. Huntington, *The Clash of Civilizations and the Remaking of World Order* (New York: Simon and Schuster, 1996), p. 125.

6. Ibid., p. 321.

ners to protect and advance the interests and values of the unique civilization they share."[7]

Huntington believes what is at stake is as follows:

> The futures of the United States and of the West depend upon Americans reaffirming their commitment to Western civilization. Domestically this means rejecting the divisive siren calls of multiculturalism. Internationally it means rejecting the elusive and illusory calls to identify the United States with Asia. Whatever economic connections may exist between them, the fundamental cultural gap between Asian and American societies precludes their joining together in a common home. Americans are culturally part of the Western family; multiculturalists may damage and even destroy that relationship but they cannot replace it. When Americans look for their cultural roots, they find them in Europe.[8]

The "clash of civilizations" and "the remaking of the world order" is a subject of concern not only to Huntington but also to Guehenno and Havel. Although all three would certainly hold different views on the validity of Huntington's theses, all would agree that the Atlantic community in 1997 is vastly different from what it was half a century ago. Europe has been transformed by the outcome of the *Cold War*. This transformation calls the *purpose* of the Atlantic community into question, as did the emerging Atlantic relationship of fifty years ago, when Europe lay in the ruins produced by the Second World War.

This transformation raises, in turn, another concern related to but different from those emphasized by Guehenno, Havel, and

---

7. As cited in William H. McNeill's review of Huntington's book, in the *New York Review of Books*, January 9, 1997, p. 19. Huntington's citation in the above quote, beginning with "adopting an Atlanticist," is found on page 312 of his book.

8. Huntington, *The Clash of Civilizations*, p. 307.

Huntington. The "clash of civilizations," the regulation of "the social clock," and the changing "world order" represent a direct challenge—in the post-1989 world—to what Austrian economist and Nobel laureate F. A. Hayek described fifty years ago as "the principal ingredients of classical liberalism"—namely,

> those values on which European civilization was built . . . the sacredness of truth . . . the ordinary rules of moral decency . . . a common belief in the value of human freedom . . . an affirmative action towards democracy . . . [and] opposition to all forms of totalitarianism, whether it be from the Right or from the Left.[9]

How strong and forceful a role these ingredients will play in the future American-European relationship places the integrity of the Atlantic community in the balance. Will its future be one of opportunism and absence of commitment to ethical standards and moral values, or will it be one of cohesion and commitment to "those values on which European civilization was built"?

There is no longer an Atlantic community in the same sense as the *military alliance* that existed from 1949 to 1989. Thus in 1989 the rationale for the alliance was still clearly definable as a treaty organization of North Atlantic countries from America (North America) and Europe (Western Europe). It existed for a single purpose: to deal with the common enemy of communist dictatorship in the Soviet Union and in Central and Eastern Europe. It was called the North Atlantic Treaty Organization, an alliance of nations with common values but often with different ways of expressing them (in English the acronym is NATO; in French it is precisely the opposite, OTAN [Organisation du traite de l'Atlantique Nord]).

Today, that tried, trying, and triumphant success called NATO

---

9. R. M. Hartwell, *A History of the Mont Pelerin Society* (Indianapolis, Ind.: Liberty Fund, 1995), p. 220.

is faced with a struggle to define new purposes, responsibilities, and obligations to share jointly.[10] To put it another way, the Atlantic community is seeking to create a new triangle of economic, political, and national security relationships of which the future of NATO is only one element. That struggle is proving more frustrating and complex than most Americans and Europeans anticipated when they celebrated the opening of the Berlin Wall. On Christmas Day 1989 television viewers in Europe and in the United States watched Leonard Bernstein change the name of Beethoven's *Ode to Joy* to *Ode to Freedom,* as he conducted the Ninth Symphony—played by musicians from France, Great Britain, the Soviet Union, and the United States, as well as from East and West Germany—in the Schauspielhaus in East Berlin. In that the Wall was the most emotional and powerful symbol of the *Cold War,* it is not difficult to understand why Berlin's 1989 celebrations on Christmas and New Year's Eve overshadowed how the end of the *Cold War* would challenge the Atlantic community as a whole and the NATO alliance in particular.

In the last seven years a great deal has been written about the future of NATO and the future of the Atlantic community. Some argue that the mutual interests of defense remain the same, even though NATO no longer confronts the conventional and nuclear forces of the Warsaw Pact. Others assert that the sense and purpose of community has changed fundamentally—that the United States has done its part for *democracy, politics, and liberty* in Europe. They conclude that the future of Europe is now the Europeans' responsibility and that maintaining the Atlantic community is no longer possible or necessary.

The challenges, however they are considered, are not simple.

---

10. The following countries belong to NATO: Belgium, Canada, Denmark, France, Germany, Greece, Iceland, Italy, Luxembourg, the Netherlands, Norway, Portugal, Spain, Turkey, the United Kingdom, the United States.

Although much within the Atlantic community has remained the same, much has changed. But it is too easy to claim, as some Americans and Europeans do, that, because the *Cold War* is over, the future of economic and political freedom in Europe is and should be of concern only to the Europeans. The political, economic, and military health of the Atlantic community may, if anything, be more important in a multipolar world of instant communication and of short-term political and economic horizons than it has been since the revolution in France more than two hundred years ago.

What both America and Europe are looking for in their future relations with each other, and with other parts of the world, is stability. But in their search thus far, both have relied on old tools and on old approaches to assess and deal with new problems. The world today, unlike the world of the *Cold War*, is not black and white but gray. To deal with its problems—whether defined by Guehenno, Hayek, Havel, or Huntington—both America and Europe need allies. They need each other because neither Europe nor America will find friends anywhere else with whom they have as much in common:

> The friendship likeliest to prove useful is the old one with Europe, often tested but always liable to be taken for granted. Four times this century—in two world wars, Korea and the Gulf—America has fought alongside Europeans. They know that undeterred aggression means war and, if they stop to think, that deterred aggression means peace: the big war they did not fight was the nuclear one with Russia. If the next 50 years are to be as relatively unbloody as the past 50, America will have to be just as resolute as it was with Soviet communism. And it will need every bit as much help from its friends.[11]

---

11. *The Economist,* November 23, 1996, p. 18.

During the past fifty years America and Europe created, celebrated, and protected the Atlantic community in an alliance that
proved to be arguably the most valuable one in this century's history of the American-European relationship. Precisely because of
Guehenno's pessimism and Huntington's warning, and exactly because of Havel's hope and Hayek's emphasis on the value of "the
principal ingredients of classical liberalism," the Atlantic community and the alliance it produced must be preserved and strengthened. To do so, the community itself must define a new raison
d'être because threats to *democracy, politics, and liberty*—to *classical
liberalism*—have not disappeared, they have just assumed new
forms.

## The Legacy of the Cold War

In Europe political, economic, and national security challenges to
the Atlantic community are represented by the questions of how
and when to expand membership of the European Union,[12] how
and when to strengthen and create new institutions such as a European Monetary Union (EMU), how and when to expand NATO
membership, how to structure NATO commands, and how to define what values the Atlantic community is committed to defend.

In North America the United States concerns itself with ques-

---

12. The fifteen members of the European Union (EU), not all of which belong
to NATO, are Austria, Belgium, Denmark, Finland, France, Germany, Greece, Ire-
land, Italy, Luxembourg, the Netherlands, Portugal, Spain, Sweden, the United
Kingdom. The following countries do not belong to the EU: Albania, Andorra,
Bulgaria, Cyprus, the Czech Republic, Estonia, Hungary, Iceland, Latvia, Liech-
tenstein, Lithuania, Malta, Norway, Poland, Romania, San Marino, the Slovak Republic, the former Soviet Union (which includes Russia and the newly independent states), Switzerland, Turkey, former Yugoslavia (which includes Slovenia). Of
the latter, several have applied for EU membership and others are members of
the European Free Trade Association (EFTA).

tions of national security as these relate not only to Europe but also to other parts of the world. Americans, just like Europeans, face domestic challenges in a wide variety of areas: budget deficits, educational quality, health and welfare programs that are draining national treasuries, tax and regulatory policies that are punitive rather than constructive, and immigration on an unprecedented scale. Both sides of the Atlantic are encountering foreign policy problems with which they do not have forty years of experience and which do not lend themselves to black-and-white solutions. Examples are ethnic conflicts, the communist legacy of environmental degradation in Central and Eastern Europe, increasing drug traffic, industrial espionage, migration and illegal immigration on a global scale, terrorism, criminal business enterprises that challenge legitimate governments, and irresponsible and dangerous behavior by governments in China, Iran, Iraq, Libya, and North Korea that do not place the same value on life and human rights as do Americans and Europeans.

One important challenge affecting the entire Atlantic community is the direct result of the investment made in Europe's future by Western Europe and America following the defeat of the Third Reich. It was an investment of hope and courage via the Marshall Plan, of defense and security via NATO, and of a commitment to the values of *classical liberalism* via American involvement with the political and economic reconstruction of Europe. That investment contributed to the collapse of communist dictatorships between 1989 and 1991 and left the Atlantic community with this question: How to build and protect democracy and free markets in Central and Eastern Europe and in the former Soviet Union so that the nightmares of tyranny and communist dictatorship do not revisit the old continent.

Part of the answer is undoubtedly found in the hopes of which Vaclav Havel wrote in mid-1996; neither challenges nor problems alone can place in jeopardy, or in question, the legitimate goal of greater prosperity and the earnest interest in preserving peace with freedom shared by the members of the Atlantic community. As a community, it is held together not by threat and adversity but by common political and philosophical values, by a commitment to the French declaration of the rights of man, and by a belief in the dignity and inviolability of the individual. These strengths hold the community together despite threats, not because of them, and despite the *Cold War*, not because of it. The events of 1989–1990 took Europe out of bondage and unified Germany, but they also raise the question of where the Atlantic community is going or, more to the point, where it should be going.

What has changed in fifty years? In 1947 Germany was a country—what was left of it—cut up into four different zones, with Berlin, its former capital, also in four sectors. The war had been over for less than two years. Today Germany is unified, and there are fewer American troops stationed there than members of united Germany's own armed forces! In 1947 the item of real value was the American cigarette—a Lucky Strike or a Camel or a Pall Mall—and the prewar free market had been replaced with a black one. In April 1947 German currency had no value; currency reform was still fourteen months away. Economic life was a nightmare. The reichsmark was useless. Today the deutsche mark is the strongest currency in Europe. In 1947 *Der Spiegel,* known fifty years later as the German equivalent of *Time* magazine, was only three months old; its first issue appeared on January 4, 1947, in Hamburg. Today, it can be found on newsstands from Berlin to London to San Francisco.

In 1947 it was inconceivable that Stalin would order the blockade of Berlin in June 1948; today Berlin is becoming the New York of Central Europe. In 1947 Berlin was "an island in the middle of a red sea" of the Soviet occupation zone; today the Soviet army is gone from Germany. In 1947, Europe was not yet divided and the western part of Germany was under military occupation by the three allied powers of England, France, and the United States. Winston Churchill, however, recognized, when he sent a telegram to Harry Truman on May 12, 1945, that "an iron curtain [has been] drawn" across Europe.[13] Reparations were moving out of Germany, and dismantling was going ahead. The distinguished German economist Wilhelm Roepke, who lived in Switzerland, concluded that "without industrial Germany being allowed to produce, the situation is disastrous."[14] In March and April 1947 the fourth meeting of the Council of Foreign Ministers, created at the Potsdam Conference in August 1945, was taking place in Moscow. The April 1 headline of the *New York Times* read, "Marshall Bars 'Ultimatum' By Soviet on Reparations; Rules Out a German 'Slum,'" and the lead article began as follows:

> Marshall flatly rejected today the Russian demand for reparations from German current production as the price of economic unity for Germany. He also told the Russians that the United States opposed policies that would make Germany a "congested slum or an economic poorhouse in the center of Europe."... [He] raised the problem of the former German territory now administered by Poland, [and] stressed the United States' desire for "one Germany."[15]

---

13. Dennis L. Bark and David R. Gress, *A History of West Germany*, 2d ed., vol. 1, *From Shadow To Substance, 1945–1963* (Oxford, Eng., and Cambridge, Mass.: Blackwell, 1993), p. 48.

14. Archives of the Mont Pelerin Society, Hoover Institution, Stanford, California.

15. The headlines of *Le Figaro* in Paris were equally telling: "Heures decisives à Moscou apres Controverse des 'Quatre' sur le Problem de l'Unité Economique de l'Allemagne" (April 1), "La Greve des Mineurs de la Ruhr est presque totale— 500,000 tonnes de Charbon perdues" (April 4), and "MM Bevin, Bidault et Marshall hostile à la proposition de M. Molotov tendant à donner aux Allemandes la liberté de choisir entre le centralisme et le federalisme" (April 8).

In 1947 more than two years would have to pass before the formation of the West German government, followed by the creation of the German Democratic Republic the following month (October 1949). Today both are gone. In 1947, the arms race had not yet begun and the Soviet Union would not explode its first atomic bomb for another two years. Today, the arms race with the former Soviet Union is over and the *Cold War* military confrontation in Europe is ended, without a shot being fired. In 1947 there was no wall dividing Berlin; it would not be built until fourteen years later. In 1997 the Wall dividing Berlin has been gone for almost eight years. What was emerging as the communist takeover of Central Europe was not yet called the *Cold War* in early 1947. Neither NATO nor the Warsaw Pact would be formed for another two years. Today the Warsaw Pact is gone. What remains is the most powerful military alliance ever built.

In early 1947 the Marshall Plan had not yet been announced and would not be until June, when the American secretary of state presented the idea in a speech at Harvard University. Fifty years later, in 1997, the funds used in what was formally known as the European Recovery Plan had been repaid to the United States. In 1947, the economic miracle was still six years away, and Ludwig Erhard, who became chancellor of West Germany in 1963, was still in the process of working out the concepts of what became known as the *social market economy;* indeed, Erhard would not be appointed to head the Special Bureau for Money and Credit until October 1947, six months later. In his wartime treatise on debt and finance, Erhard had boldly written that only a free market system could solve the problems of physical devastation and worthless money that were easily foreseeable in 1943–1944, but in the smoking ruins of Europe's cities a different view prevailed:

Most Europeans in 1945 [in 1947 as well] regarded socialism, or at least some form of extensive state control of the economy, as so obviously necessary as to be beyond argument. Socialists argued that it would lead both to greater social justice and to much greater efficiency . . . only under state control could the industrial economies possibly handle the overwhelming national and international problems of the postwar period.[16]

It was not difficult to understand why that opinion was widespread in war-torn Europe. The message was simply and powerfully conveyed in a graffito scrawled on the wall of a Berlin apartment building in the spring of 1945: "Enjoy the war—the peace is going to be terrible."[17] In occupied Germany living from one day to the next was a complicated matter. The economic blame was cast on the prewar free market, which, it was widely held, produced Hitler's war machine built by German firms like Krupp. Indeed, the *four d*'s used by the four victors to describe occupation policy in Germany began with *de*cartelization, and continued with *de*nazification, *de*militarization, and *de*mocratization (*de*centralization was added, depending on where you read the description).

If a coup de grâce was necessary, the distinguished British historian A. J. P. Taylor provided it after the war, when he asserted that

nobody in Europe believes in the American way of life—that is, in private enterprise; or rather those who believe it are a defeated party and a party which seems to have no more future than the Jacobites in England after 1688.[18]

Taylor's views, however, were not given a great deal of credence by the new Christian Democratic Party (CDU) in the western zones of occupied Germany, of which both West Germany's first chan-

---

16. Bark and Gress, *History of West Germany*, vol. 1, p. 193.
17. Ibid., p. 5.
18. Ibid., p. 193.

cellor, Konrad Adenauer, and Erhard were members. In what was to represent a decisive step in the development of the CDU's economic policy, the party approved an economic program in the town of Ahlen in Westphalia in February 1947:

> The new structure of the German economy must proceed from the assumption that the time of unlimited power of private capitalism is over. But we must also avoid replacing private capitalism with state capitalism, which would be even more dangerous for the political and economic freedom of the individual. A new economic structure must be sought which avoids the mistakes of the past and which allows the possibility of technical progress and creative initiative of the individual.[19]

This declaration was close to revolutionary in 1947, given prevailing views of national socialism's contribution to the destruction of Europe and the blanket condemnation of capitalism as a principal cause of the evils of the Third Reich. Indeed, the economic program of the Social Democratic Party (SPD), which had been forbidden in Nazi Germany and reconstituted in the western zones of occupation, had been approved in Hannover in May 1946. That program read, in part, as follows:

> Today's Germany is no longer in the position to carry a private, capitalistic profit-economy, and to pay profits from exploitation, capital dividends and bond income. . . . Just as socialism without democracy is not possible, so is, on the contrary, democracy in a capitalistic state in continuous danger. On the basis of these special historical circumstances and the characteristics of the intellectual development in Germany, German democracy needs socialism. German democracy must be socialist, or the counterrevolutionary forces will destroy it once again.[20]

---

19. Ibid., p. 196.
20. Ibid., pp. 195–96.

The SPD's program appealed to people who did not have enough to eat, who had no currency of value, who had no job, and who could not travel from one zone of occupation to another without permission. Those trials and tribulations, although the Germans and the Europeans did not know it, were going to continue for a very long time. In fact, there was no end in sight. Erhard, for his part, maintained a steady course, successfully framed in the Ahlen program—until he announced, in June 1948, the decision taken by the Economic Council of the three western zones to abolish price controls, rationing and introduce, at the same time, a new currency. The American and British commanding generals, Lucius Clay and Sir Brian Robertson, were appalled. Clay called Erhard to Frankfurt and the following conversation ensued:

> "Herr Erhard, my advisors tell me that what you have done is a terrible mistake. What do you say to that?"
> . . ."Herr General, pay no attention to them! My own advisors tell me the same thing."[21]

The wisdom of currency reform may seem self-evident, in the light of half a century's passing, but the advantages of a stable currency were far from clear to the Germans in June 1948. One of the most telling descriptions of what it all meant was written by Richard Tuengel, a journalist in postwar Germany who became an editor in chief of *Die Zeit* in Hamburg:

> For a journalist like me it [the currency reform] approached like a steamroller. It made me tremble with fear, and I was convinced that it would crush me. In reality the currency reform . . . ap-

---

21. Ibid., p. 202.

proached like a wave, carrying singing dolphins. The wave took us in and carried us absolutely gently forward.[22]

The decision to reform the currency took great courage (as it did forty-two years later in 1990, when Chancellor Helmut Kohl exchanged East German currency for West German currency at a one-to-one ratio, against the advice of financial experts including the chairman of the Bundesbank in Frankfurt, Otto Poehl). At the same time, Adenauer—who was not called *Der Alte* for nothing— and Erhard knew exactly what they were doing and did it! They had laid the groundwork with the Ahlen program and followed it sixteen months later with the power of the currency reform. They both were preparing the way for the German voters to make a choice between a market economy, including *the values of classical liberalism*, and what was euphemistically described as a planned economy. The voters in the three western zones of occupation made that choice in September 1949.

*The values of classical liberalism*, however, were not universally championed on the continent, as attested to by the views of A. J. P. Taylor. F. A. Hayek considered discussion of the importance of these values, as they would be incorporated in the reconstruction of *democracy, politics, and liberty* in postwar Europe, to be fundamental. It was with this concern in mind that thirty-nine individuals met from April 1 to 10, 1947, in the village of Mont Pelerin, Switzerland, at his invitation, to discuss them. The group, consisting of men who would play a major role in building *democracy, politics, and liberty* in the post–World War II world, included Karl Brandt, Walter Eucken, Milton Friedman, T. J. B. Hoff, Carl Iversen, John Jewkes, Frank Knight, H. de Lovinfosse, Fritz Machlup, Loren B. Miller, Ludwig von Mises, Felix Morley, Michael Polanyi, Karl Popper, William Rappard, Lionel Robbins, Wilhelm Roepke,

---

22. Ibid., p. 201.

Walter Ruestow, Fritz Schnabel, George Stigler, and Francis Tre-
voux. Out of that meeting emerged the Mont Pelerin Society,
whose members shared a commitment to the values of *classical
liberalism*, as defined by Hayek. Those founding members expressed their concern with economic freedom and individual liberty as follows:

> The position of the individual and the voluntary group is pro-
> gressively undermined by extensions of arbitrary power. . . . The
> group holds that these developments have been fostered by the
> growth of a view of history which denies all absolute moral stan-
> dards and by the growth of theories which question the desira-
> bility of the rule of law . . . that they have been fostered by a de-
> cline of belief in private property and the competitive market.[23]

Bound tightly to the future of Germany was the future of Europe. In 1947, as now, the future of both went hand in hand. One
goal of the occupying powers was to reconstruct a Germany that
would never again pose a military threat to Europe. One goal of a
united Germany fifty years later, and so expressed by German leaders on numerous occasions since 1990, is that the Germans, after
forty years of division, seek to build a European Germany, not a
German Europe.

In history books and in newspapers one has read, again and
again since 1989, that the *Cold War* was dangerous, that the threat
of nuclear conflict cast a pall over the efforts of post–World War II
diplomats to deal with the questions of peace and war. That may
be true, and one can rest assured that historians will argue the
point for decades. It is also true that the *Cold War* contained, ironically, elements of predictability that have disappeared. Of vastly
greater significance, however, is that the certainties of dictatorship

---

23. "Summary of History and Aims," archives of the Mont Pelerin Society, Hoover Institution Archives.

were replaced with freedom of choice, with German unification, and with an end to the division of Europe into armed camps.

It is also true that relations among European states, and between Europe and the United States, have become more argumentative, more difficult to manage, and in some cases unstable and violent, for example, the former Yugoslavia, Chechnya, and the tensions between Turkey and Greece over Cyprus. More important, both American and European leaders have been unable to define and agree on common approaches to these new problems. Yugoslavia is a tragic illustration. Political leaders on both continents have agreed, however, on several consequences of the end of the *Cold War,* namely, that different threats and risks have replaced old ones, creating new vulnerabilities. Three of those new vulnerabilities were defined by Margaret Thatcher at a meeting held in Prague in May 1996 at which the subject was the Atlantic community. Lady Thatcher's description was as follows:

> First of all, there was a kind of unholy symmetry in international affairs created by a balance of terror. Neither the West nor the Soviets could afford to let any regional crisis so destabilize the system that either side was pushed to the brink; for beyond that brink lay the abyss of mutual destruction. The breakdown of Soviet power, however, brought that discipline to an end; it allowed irresponsible states, often connected with terrorist movements, to emerge and set their own violent agendas.
>
> Second, with the collapse of the Soviet Union there was also a dispersal of weapons of mass destruction. This has gone much further than we envisaged, and it now constitutes quite simply the most dangerous threat of our times. . . .
>
> Third, we are seeing today a fundamental shift of economic power—which will certainly have political consequences—away from the West to Asia and the Pacific Rim. The danger lies in the fact that these Asian countries generally lack the liberal traditions which we in the West take for granted. America is worthy of its superpower status because it has been not only economically but

politically liberal. By contrast, China's extraordinary economic progress is occurring despite, not because of, its political tradition—which has always been one of tyranny.[24]

The changes that have engulfed Europe since 1989 continue to affect the Atlantic community. Whereas there were 340,000 American troops in Western Europe at the end of 1989, in early 1997 there were only about 100,000. Whereas there was a clear American commitment to the defense of Berlin, Western Germany, and Western Europe, that commitment is no longer necessary. Whereas there was no dispute about what united the Atlantic community—namely, the defense of freedom—today that freedom is no longer threatened by communist military dictatorships. Whereas today much of the European continent is free, that freedom does not by definition unify the Atlantic community. Whereas American foreign policy interests vis-à-vis Europe were always a major subject of any presidential election campaign in the United States, for the first time since 1945 it was not so during the 1996 political debates between President Clinton and Senator Dole. So, for example, in the autumn of 1996, former Secretary of State Henry Kissinger participated in a panel of eight, four Democrats and four Republicans. For two and a half hours they discussed election campaign issues. During that period Kissinger was the only panel member to raise foreign policy questions of importance to the United States, that is to say, for twelve and a half minutes out of two and a half hours.[25]

There is a message here, and it is not a happy one. European issues are no longer on the daily agenda of American politics as

---

24. Margaret Thatcher, "The West after the Cold War," *Wall Street Journal,* May 14, 1996.

25. From remarks entitled "Handlungsfaehigkeit fuer Europa," presented at a symposium held in Berlin on October 30, 1996, "Schoenhauser Gespraeche: Das Vierte Gesellschaftspolitisches Forum der Banken."

they once were, even though there are issues, as Lady Thatcher
defined them, of critical importance to both continents. Changes
in Europe and shifting policy priorities in the United States do not
mean that relations between the "old country" and the "new
world" are falling apart. But, as far as relations between America
and Europe are concerned, mutual agreement on how to define
and address common interests has become more difficult to
achieve.

The Atlantic community, seen from the perspective of 1997,
presents a landscape Americans and Europeans have awaited for
more than half the twentieth century. Europe is no longer Western Europe. It is all of Europe. The nature and composition of the
Atlantic community is changing. But although change brings new
problems, today's challenges on both sides of the Atlantic are the
consequences of freedom and success, not the products of tyranny
and failure. *The values of classical liberalism* and their role in the
conduct of the affairs of the civilized world are, however, being
challenged once again.

## Europe, Economic Power, and Maastricht

The absence in America of consistent, responsible, public discussion and debate of the international issues facing both continents
should trouble Americans as well as Europeans. The lack of debate—at least until the appointment of Madeleine Albright as U.S.
secretary of state in January 1997—raises a basic question: How
will Europe and America relate to each other in the future?[26] The
significance of this question is reflected in the changing nature of

---

26. This question was also raised by Henry Kissinger in Berlin in his remarks
of October 30, 1996.

the European Union (EU).[27] The movement to build a federation of Europe—a European Union—which has been under way since the Marshall Plan, continues forward, and it is not at all clear how and where it will end. This movement is illustrated by the following milestones:

1951    The Treaty of Paris establishes the European Coal and Steel Community (ECSC).

1957    The Treaty of Rome establishes the European Economic Community (EEC) and the European Atomic Energy Commission (EURATOM).

1960    The Stockholm Convention establishing the European Free Trade Association (EFTA) is signed.

1979    The European Monetary System (EMS) begins operation.

1985    Jacques Delors is appointed president of the (European) Commission.

1986    The Single European Act is signed; introduced on January 1, 1993, the act reduces or eliminates physical, tax, and technical barriers.

1989    Delors is reappointed president of the (European) Commission for a further four years.

1990    The agreement establishing the European Bank for Reconstruction and Development is signed in Paris.

1990    The Schengen Agreement on the elimination of border checks is signed.

1992    The Maastricht Treaty on European Union is signed, which establishes the criteria for creation of a central bank and introduction of a common currency—the euro—on January 1, 1999.

---

27. See note 12.

1993    The single market goes into effect on January 1, and the EU is created in accordance with the terms of the Maastricht Treaty.

1995    The EU is enlarged from twelve to fifteen members (in a referendum Norway's voters reject entry).

1997    The Intergovernmental Conference (representatives from the EU) meets to discuss issues related to creation of the European Monetary Union (a common currency and a central bank).

These milestones, and the union they are creating, raise a second challenge of fundamental importance. If the Atlantic community is concerned with building and protecting democracy and free markets in Central and Eastern Europe and in the former Soviet Union, so must it also be concerned with how to protect free markets in Western Europe from the stifling embrace of the welfare state—which, by definition, threatens *the values of classical liberalism.*

Why is protecting free markets just as important as protecting democracy? Consider the following example. The commitment to strengthen the institutions of the European Union (EU), which is represented by the Maastricht Treaty of 1992, is the means by which the EU is seeking to deal with Europe's economic and political future. Many European states are being strangled by taxes of all kinds and by social security costs and labor laws that make it extremely expensive to add new employees and dismiss unproductive ones. In early 1997 the EU's unemployment rate was twice that of the United States. A study on "Economic Freedom," published at the end of 1996 jointly by the *Wall Street Journal* and the Heritage Foundation, "puts 19 countries ahead of Germany and 30 ahead of France in the degree of freedom from government-imposed economic burdens."[28]

---

28. "Europe's Year of Reckoning," *Wall Street Journal*, December 27, 1996.

Exorbitant tax rates and uncompetitive labor costs as well as growing government deficits and debt in France and Germany, to cite two examples, cannot continue without highly destructive economic and political effects. Yet when individual European leaders seek to cut budgets (which means reducing social program benefits) or try to deal firmly with labor unions (as during the French railway strike in the autumn of 1996) or seek to reduce sick leave compensation from 100 percent of salary to 80 percent (as in Germany during the autumn of 1996) or explain that government salaries and benefits must be reduced because they exceed those of private enterprise, whose profits provide the taxes to pay government salaries and benefits (as in France and Italy), they are met with riots in the streets and defeat at the ballot box. Confronted with what can only be described as the public and private sectors at loggerheads, most European political leaders, as would most American leaders, easily read the signals.

If Europe's leaders try to limit the size of social programs, and urge deficit reduction and balanced budgets, they do so at the peril of their political lives. Government "austerity" proposals are met by truck strikes that tie up French and Spanish highways and by work stoppages and high unemployment in Germany. The result is that European political leaders do not want to tell their respective voters the truth, which is that most of the members of the EU, particularly France, Germany, Italy, and Sweden, are overtaxed, overregulated, overgoverned, and overspent.

Since European leaders seem to be unable to reduce taxes and government expenditures by appealing to their electorates, they are seeking to use the Maastricht Treaty to do so. Following the introduction of the single market on January 1, 1993, the treaty set forth the conditions for the introduction of the European Monetary Union on January 1, 1999, in other words, creation of a single currency—the *euro*—and a central bank. French and German government leaders are seeking to cut the onerous costs of massive social programs by citing the necessity to meet the three primary criteria established in the treaty that govern adoption and use of a single European currency, namely, (1) government deficits shall not exceed 3 percent of gross domestic product (GDP), (2) gross debt shall not exceed 60 percent of GDP, and (3) the annual rate of inflation shall not exceed 1.5 percent of the average of the three best-performing states during the previous year. Thus, emphasis on meeting the terms of the treaty, while seriously meant, also masks major economic problems with which few European political leaders wish to deal alone because they are afraid of being voted out of office.

It is uncertain at this point how successful they will be in their efforts to honor the treaty. It is forecast for 1997, for example, that only Luxembourg, of the fifteen EU members, will meet the inflation, deficit, and debt requirements[29] (France may as well, although only because of a creative accounting transfer that moved the future value of France-Telecom pension fund obligations into the government budget). In contrast, EU monetary commissioner Yves-Thibault de Silguy felt confident enough to announce in early November 1996 that "the financial markets no longer have any doubt that the euro will exist as of January 1, 1999."[30] He also predicted that twelve of the EU members would have budget deficits below 3 percent of GDP in 1997 and that ten would meet the inflation criterion.

Obviously, in such predictions there is a good deal of politics mixed into the batter, which undoubtedly is wise, given the deadline the Maastricht Treaty sets. Any way it is counted, however, the EU's members have a long way to go to put their respective houses

---

29. "Austria," *Country Report, 4th Quarter* (Economist Intelligence Unit), December 1996, p. 17.

30. *The Week In Germany*, November 8, 1996.

in order if they are to meet their schedule. According to an editorial in the *Wall Street Journal* at the end of December 1996,

> Utopian dreams of prosperity haven't been realized because there is a big difference between a free market and the "single market." In return for bringing down barriers to trade between European states (which were already quite low), Europeans got thousands of new barriers to trade from bureaucrats in Brussels. Businesses were now "free" to trade throughout the EU, but only if they could bear the costs of mandated paperwork, new testing and certification requirements, and onerous "social" regulations. . . . In our view, there is nothing about the single currency, or any other part of European integration, that can substitute for necessary structural reforms in Europe's welfare states. Massive unfunded pension debts, rigid labor markets and bloated state bureaucracies will continue to be a drag on economic growth and employment no matter how much harmonizing is done.[31]

Both Europeans and Americans should pay close attention to what Maastricht represents. It is nothing less than the attempt by Western European governments to change Europe's economic relationship not only with America but with the rest of the world as well, in addition to serving as a means of dealing with unprecedented social and welfare costs. There is a lot riding on the outcome.

How quickly the EU will become more competitive, and at what sacrifice to individual liberty, is an unresolved question. The EU, however, does make up the world's largest potential market, with a gross domestic product of $8.4 trillion dollars, 20 percent larger than that of the United States.[32] American business and political leaders should pay more attention than they have thus far to the significance of economic competition from a European

---

31. "Europe's Year of Reckoning."
32. "A Survey of Business in Europe," *The Economist*, November 23, 1996, p. 4.

Union that is likely to have only one bank and one currency, instead of fifteen of each. From an American viewpoint the prospect of greater economic competition from Europe should be welcomed because American business is capable of meeting the challenge in a competitive and constructive way. To do so, however, it must recognize that future challenges exist not only in the free marketplace of commerce but also in the arena of *democracy, politics, and liberty,* where ideas compete with one another. Will the values of *classical liberalism* prevail as the terms of the Maastricht Treaty are transformed, step by step, into real policies? It is still an open question!

Whatever may be the consequences of greater European Union, they will be felt not only in America but also in countries throughout the world. Consider, for example, the following from an article written by William Pfaff in December 1996:

> If the future euro trades at a level that reflects relative domestic purchasing power, and if international trade becomes increasingly denominated in euros, this will make trouble for U.S. businessmen and consumers. Yves Galland, France's minister delegate for finance and foreign trade, says he is certain that "the euro will very rapidly become the leading world money, let's say in 15 or 20 years."[33]

That conclusion, which is obviously debatable, focuses directly on the reality of "Maastricht" itself. European leaders to the contrary, it is not clear that a majority of Europeans think abolishing national currencies is a good idea; nor is it clear that a majority supports one currency with the name of *euro* or a central bank located in Frankfurt. Given the extremely close results of the national referenda held in Europe during 1992 and 1993, opinion

---

33. William Pfaff, "Many Worry That the Euro Could Break Europe, Not Make It," *International Herald Tribune,* December 9, 1996.

among the Europeans on the wisdom of the Maastricht Treaty is split more or less down the middle.

"Maastricht," moreover, means different things to different people, for varied political and economic reasons. The Germans seek a European Germany, not a German Europe, to build European confidence in united Germany's position in Central Europe. One vehicle that can provide that confidence is the Maastricht Treaty. The French seek a Germany that will be kept in political and economic balance, vis-à-vis its neighbors, within a European Union. The treaty is a step in that direction. The British object to neither balance nor a European Germany, but "Eurosceptics" in Britain, as journalists have been quick to call them, do have misgivings about the European Monetary Union. They also see in the Maastricht Treaty an effort by Western European Socialists, led by French socialist Jacques Delors, to *socialize* Europe via the *backdoor* of the European Commission and Brussels bureaucracy (following the setback delivered to the appeal of socialism by the behavior of communist dictatorships). None of these considerations, however, are likely to prevent the introduction of one currency or the creation of a central bank.

How it will all work, however, is another matter. To illustrate, let us look at the operation of the European Commission, located in Brussels. The commission has a full-time staff of about sixteen thousand directed by twenty commissioners. Its influence was most powerfully felt in 1990–1991, when Jacques Delors was pushing the "single-market programme" that resulted in the signing of the Maastricht Treaty in 1992. Delors, at that point, felt confident enough to "forecast a time when 80% of social and economic legislation in Europe would come from Brussels,"[34] which in turn produced the debates that continue today concerning the power

---

34. "The Big Squeeze," *The Economist,* February 8, 1997, pp. 55–56.

exercised by unelected commission bureaucrats, unaccountable to Europe's voters.

By 1996 it appeared that the nature of the commission had begun to change. Its activity had significantly slowed down; in 1995 it made only twelve new legislative proposals and withdrew almost fifty. Indeed, Erkki Liikanen, the Finnish budget commissioner, commented, critically, that "the commission mixes the traditions of 'French hierarchy, German *Mitbestimmung* [codetermination] and Italian trade unions.'"[35] An analysis in *The Economist* in February 1997 concluded that "the allocation of top jobs, especially the 25 directors-general, often degenerates into a nightmare of lobbying, inserting senior officials and filling unspoken nationality quotas in which the ability to do the job is forgotten."[36] What these developments mean, however, is still unclear.

Problems also are evident in the operation of the European Parliament. It conducts its affairs in eleven different languages, has 626 elected members, and transacts business in three different locations: Strasbourg for monthly meetings, Brussels for committee sessions and "miniplenaries," and the offices of its 3,800-member secretariat in Luxembourg. This allocation of responsibility costs approximately $124 million annually in rent and travel expenses. The parliament is charged with exercising "democratic control" over the European Commission, but the national governments of the EU's members choose the commissioners. Moreover, the parliament's members are elected in campaigns that tend to focus on national, not European, issues, and in France, Italy, and Spain, for example, a "list system" is used that provides "no link between a Euro-MP and his constituency." Thus, the parliament is, to quote *The Economist,*

---

35. Ibid.
36. Ibid.

a body that few of the Union's 370 [million] citizens recognize,
let alone love. One reason is that its job is misunderstood. Most
voters expect an elected parliament to produce a government
and to function in an adversarial way. The European Parliament
does neither. . . . It needs consensus among its political groups to
create absolute majorities to amend laws. It tends to work in ca-
hoots with the commission [which has the exclusive right to propose legislation].[37]

So, where does this leave the Atlantic community in 1997? The
movement for a greater European federation will continue. With
the assistance of the Maastricht Treaty, the Europeans are going
to create or expand (or both) bureaucratic institutions that re-
strict the liberty of the individual but that are intended to create a
true free market on the continent for the first time in European
history. Out of this effort will emerge a greater degree of European economic and political integration than exists today. At some
point Poland, the Czech Republic, and Hungary, in addition to
other European states, will also be included.

Of critical concern, however, is what the EU will become, and
how it will influence post-1989 *democracy, politics, and liberty* in Europe. Who will make the rules? Who will play the leading roles?
Through it all Germany will be in the middle, whether it likes it or
not; it is not an accident that the European Central Bank will be
in Frankfurt. Why? Germany has a vested interest in seeing the
emergence of what Chancellor Kohl has repeatedly described,
since 1990, as a European Germany, not a German Europe. Germany's neighbors also wish to see Germany anchored firmly in the
European political and economic union and wish to see Germany
playing a responsible role in NATO. This is not surprising since
Germany has played a major role, since 1949, in the effort to
preserve economic and political freedom in Western Europe.

37. "Looking for Legitimacy," *The Economist,* January 11, 1997, pp. 49–50.

That effort, to which the Western Europeans and the United States have committed so many resources since 1947, has been in many ways eminently successful. To paraphrase Winston Churchill, however, success is never final.

## Economic Opportunities and Political Rivalries

There exist, in *post–Cold War* Europe, tremendous economic opportunities as well as difficult political rivalries. More and more businesses are becoming international in scope—a scholar in California can order a book from Basil Blackwell in Oxford, England, via electronic mail or a fax machine. A Parisian with a Visa or American Express card can order CD music discs on the World Wide Web from a company located in Fremont, California— *www.mass-music.com*—any day of the week, day or night, for delivery within the next five days. An antique buyer in Chicago, using the World Wide Web, can make a bid at an auction held in Vienna's venerable Dorotheum. More and more international business meetings will take place with less travel and fewer hotel stays, with less driving and less gasoline consumption, because of the growing ease of arranging meetings via video conference. New communication technology, with both its strengths and its weaknesses, makes the concept of a common economic and political destiny for America and Europe more relevant, not less so. One thing the Internet world of e-mail, fax, and cellular telephone (which was forbidden under communist dictatorship) cannot do, however, is persuade its Internet beneficiaries that the cornerstones of free markets are *the values of classical liberalism*—values to which not everyone subscribes and threats to which not everyone understands.

European as well as Asian stock markets are becoming marketplaces of the world, which they were not just ten years ago—when their "backrooms" were still doing much of their accounting with pencils and electronic access to trading on foreign stock exchanges was difficult. All that has changed. The Internet makes the divide between continents smaller, in both economic and political terms. For American and European bankers, stockbrokers, and investment houses, the Internet means that more people will have access to broader financial markets at less cost. What the revolution in communication technology means for global markets today, and will mean tomorrow, is illustrated by the amount of money American institutions are now committing to investment in stock and bond markets abroad. The statistics speak for themselves:

- In 1997 American investors owned more than $800 billion in foreign stocks and bonds, an increase from $109 billion in 1985.[38]

- U.S. institutional assets invested overseas grew from $3 billion in 1980 to $367 billion at the end of 1996 in U.S. dollar terms.

- Total institutional assets invested overseas as a percent of total assets were in the area of 1–2 percent in the early 1980s. This increased to the 11 percent area at the end of 1996.[39]

- "Foreign outlays by U.S. institutional investors should rise $150 billion to some $517 billion in the three years through

38. This statistic is from the Securities Industry Association, as cited in the *Wall Street Journal*, March 4, 1997.

39. This information was provided by Richard P. Kost, International Equities Fund Management, First Chicago/NBD Corporation, as was the information concerning foreign outlays by U.S. institutional investors cited in the next entry, taken from an article by Margaret Price, "Foreign Investments Grow," *Pensions and Investments*, January 1997.

1999.... As of 1996, 76 % of investors—including an average of 85 % of endowments—said they already invested abroad. Another 20 % said they planned to start investing internationally in the next 12 months. If borne out, that would bring to 96 % the number of institutions with foreign holdings."

If there are new economic opportunities, there are also new political rivalries. Unlike economic competition, which is healthy, political rivalry among allies can produce unwelcome outcomes, such as Charles de Gaulle's decision to leave NATO in the 1960s. Between 1949 and 1989 the European role in Western Europe's defense was limited since the United States held command of NATO's nuclear forces and also had almost 600,000 American soldiers, dependents, and civilian military employees in Europe. In 1997 United States' forces and weapons systems no longer play the dominant role. But nuclear weapons have not been removed from Europe; more than twenty thousand still exist in Russia, and independent nuclear forces exist in both France and the United Kingdom. In France, Germany, and the United Kingdom, the armed forces are all larger than those of the United States in Europe. Today, if the military alliance is to be credible as well as workable, it must be equal in the sense that responsibility is shared. This is a political issue of the post-1989 world, not simply a military one.

The attention Europeans are giving this concern is not misplaced, nor should it be construed as *anti-American*. If the Atlantic community is to provide leadership, its members must do so together and take responsibility together for the quality of their leadership. This point applies especially to the responsibility for NATO's principal military commands. The position of secretary-general of NATO, whose headquarters, Supreme Headquarters Allied Powers Europe (SHAPE), are located in Evere, near Brussels, is held by different NATO members on an elective basis; the current secretary-general is from Spain. Under SHAPE are NATO's two strategic commands, the Atlantic Command (SACLANT), located in Norfolk, Virginia, and the European Command (SACEUR), located in Casteau, Belgium. Both commands were always held by American officers during the *Cold War* and continue to be held by American officers; at some future time, however, the question of placing the European Command under the direction of a European will be raised. Finally, under the European Command there are three regional commands, the Northwest Region, commanded by a British officer, the Central Region, commanded by a German officer, and the Southern Region, commanded by an American officer.

In the autumn of 1996 French president Jacques Chirac requested that the Southern Command be assigned to a European flag officer. An editorial writer of the *New York Times* argued as follows on its editorial page:

> Washington is right to insist that an American admiral hold this job, which includes control over the United States Sixth Fleet. . . . NATO's top officer for Europe, by tradition an American, has three regional deputies. A British officer generally commands the Northwestern region, a German runs the Central region and an American is in charge of the South. Citing traditional French interests in the Mediterranean area, Mr. Chirac has demanded the Southern Command.
>
> That is a job no American President can or should yield. The Southern Commander effectively directs the formidable naval and air resources the United States has based in the Mediterranean area. In addition to their NATO responsibilities, these units are used to project American power into the Middle East, where United States and French policies do not always coincide.[40]

---

40. December 5, 1996.

If there is something to be learned from that editorial, it is that America and Europe must reassess and change their political relationship with each other in as fundamental a way as the communication revolution is beginning to change economic interests on both continents. The United States, no longer directing the conduct of the *Cold War*, now maintains a vastly reduced military presence in Europe as a consequence, as the French president rightly pointed out in his request for a European officer to hold the Southern Command.

The United States cannot have it both ways, nor, by any stretch of the imagination, do all American leaders want to have it both ways. But a large element of American pride is bound up in its historical role in the defense of freedom in Europe. Many Americans feel, with some justification, that, during two world wars, their participation and that of their forefathers who rest in European cemeteries have earned them a permanent voice in European affairs. Thus, it is one thing for Europeans to endorse shared and equal responsibilities and quite another for American representatives and senators to explain it in a way that makes sense to their constituents, many of whom are veterans. The Europeans must understand this difficulty because and in spite of the changing nature of the Atlantic community.

On the one hand, the United States welcomes the French decision to rejoin NATO as a part of the restructuring process "to redesign the alliance to insure the security and stability of Europe and American economic and political interests . . . in the changed geopolitical environment of the 21st century."[41] So editorialized the *New York Times* on December 5, 1996: "Bringing French forces back into NATO would mean a stronger alliance and a better balance between European and American military contributions

---

41. Craig R. Whitney, "French Demand That U.S. Pass Control to European Commander Delays NATO Restructuring," *New York Times*, December 3, 1996.

to the common defense. . . . To secure these benefits, Washington should seek agreement on an appropriate way to satisfy France's reasonable ambition to join NATO's top command structure." This is exactly the point, but even the *New York Times* succumbs to *the having-it-both-ways temptation;* earlier in the same editorial the writer had criticized the French proposal.[42]

It is in the interest of Europeans and Americans to share responsibility in a way that was not possible during the *Cold War.* It is, for example, neither logical nor desirable to justify American flag officers holding major command posts if the only rationale for doing so is "by tradition," to quote the *New York Times.* Joint responsibility means joint command. Both Europe and the United States have to understand that, and act on it, irrespective, for example, of whether French and American policy in the Middle East always coincides.

The French foreign minister, Herve de Charette, put the issue very well in discussing the Southern Command furor in December 1996:[43]

> *It is not true that France wants a French officer* [italics added] at the head of the southern command. France wants the . . . regional European commands assigned to European officers on a rotating basis. Since the United States insists that the two supreme commanders at the strategic level, to whom the regional commanders answer, should remain Americans, it seems fair enough that the Europeans assume significant responsibilities at the next command level. . . .
>
> It is not true that France wants the 6th Fleet to come under foreign command. The new political and strategic realities in Europe amply justify that regional commands be manned by Eu-

---

42. See the reference in the earlier paragraph from the same editorial of December 5, 1996.

43. Herve de Charette, "France for a Stream Lined NATO. Setting the Record Straight," *New York Times,* December 10, 1996.

ropean officers, but we are aware of the special strategic role played by the 6th Fleet, a key instrument not only for NATO missions but also for the defense of American national interests.

We have always made clear that arrangements should be devised to allow the fleet to stay under a purely American chain of command, even when the southern command is assumed by a European. . . .

What it all boils down to is that France, supported by some other key European partners, deems it necessary, since the United States keeps the two strategic command positions, that the next level of command in Europe be attributed to European officers on a rotating basis, while deferring to key U.S. interests in the Mediterranean.

My fear at present is that forces of conservatism and nostalgia might be gaining ground on both sides of the Atlantic.

France is committed to fully participating in a new NATO, in which the Europeans assume a proper share of the burdens and responsibilities, and which opens up to the new democracies to our east while framing a new relationship with Russia.

For us not to miss these opportunities, we need our political vision of the future to steer the debate, not forces of the past.

The United States must decide, together with its European allies, what the various and different roles in European defense should be. Indeed, concerning the French proposal, the United States should welcome it. Of NATO's fourteen European members (excluding Canada and the United States), France has made a realistic proposal to share responsibility in a practical way.

As the worlds of the international marketplace and political responsibility change, so too does the world of national security. A former director of Northern European Affairs in the Department of State argues as follows:

NATO will survive into the next century as the primary vehicle for organizing security in Europe, albeit in greater concern politically with the EU and the Organization for Security and Cooperation in Europe (OSCE) and reorganized militarily to meet the threat that all now agree is more likely—brushfire intrastate ethnic conflicts on the southeastern fringes of the continent.[44]

If that argument is true, then the absence of American concern with foreign affairs, so evident in the 1996 national election, bodes ill for America and for Europe, especially in view of the following conclusion:

> There is . . . considerable agreement within Europe—including Moscow—that continued and even expanded American involvement is needed to ensure success [in dealing with "ethnic turmoil"]. But there remains precious little consensus in the United States about such American involvement.
>
> This is the central question about the prospects for European security. Despite its centrality, it is a question that generally is curiously absent from current analyses. It hovers over those analyses like a fearsome specter to be avoided. Fearsome because of the growing suspicion that Americans may answer the question with a resounding "no!" It is a question that must be answered in the affirmative.[45]

Unlike the period of the *Cold War*, the Atlantic community of our future cannot be dominated by the United States if the relationship is to serve America and Europe well. This means that America and Europe will not always agree, as in the current debate about whether a European or American flag officer should head NATO's Southern Command or in the U.S. trade embargo against Cuba, which threatens economic sanctions against European and Canadian firms doing business with that country.

If America, and Americans, welcomes the unity of Germany

---

44. Victor Gray, "U.S. Role in European Defense," *San Francisco Chronicle,* January 6, 1997.
45. Ibid.

and embraces newly won freedoms in Central and Eastern Europe and in the former Soviet Union, it must also accept all the consequences, not just some of them. Arguing the logic of shared responsibility by citing "tradition," as the *New York Times* did in its December editorial, is not a vote of confidence in either America or Europe. And it should not surprise American leaders if the Europeans do not like it. One could argue, and it was so argued on countless occasions throughout the *Cold War*, that if America bore the primary responsibility for the defense of Berlin, Western Germany, and Western Europe as a whole, then it also had the responsibility to provide the military leadership, which it did. But that period is ended, passed over by both time and technology.

## Common Sense and Good Foreign Policy

Common concerns and shared responsibilities produce a community of interests. In the case of the Atlantic community there is a great deal to draw on. Lady Thatcher put it well from both a European and an American perspective:

> the task we face now is to devise a framework of international cooperation which allows . . . future threats to be met successfully. It is one which requires principle and shrewdness, tenacity and flexibility, resolve to apply our strength but prudence in conserving it. Above all, it requires the unity of the West under American leadership.
>
> In recent years we have heard repeated suggestions that the West [another word for the Atlantic community] was essentially a Cold War construct, rendered irrelevant by the end of a bipolar world. In fact, it was—and is—nothing of the sort. The distinctive features of the Western political, judicial, social and economic system existed before communism and will continue after it. Those features are: the long-standing historic commitment to

human rights, the rule of law, representative democracy, limited government, private property and tolerance.

Attempts today to suggest that American civilization is antithetical and antipathetic to European civilization, which itself is portrayed by contrast as some homogenous whole, are bad history and worse politics. American civilization began its life as a branch of the English oak. It has since had the cultures and traditions of other European countries grafted onto it. In truth America is a European power—and must remain one. Any ideology that threatens Atlantic unity is one that ultimately imperils our collective security.[46]

What Europe will look like in the future requires a long-term view because there are a great many more milestones along the way to whatever Europe becomes. For America, traveling this path *with* Europe makes more sense than watching it from a distance. That means paying more attention to what the Europeans are trying to do as they wrestle with strengthening and enlarging their economic and political union.

America's new secretary of state, Madeleine Albright, born in Czechoslovakia, put the case very well in January 1997: "It is a central lesson of this century that America must remain a European power . . . European stability depends in large measure on continued American engagement and leadership. And as history attests, European stability is also vital to our national interests."[47] Indeed, Albright is giving substance to her conviction, as illustrated by her meetings with French foreign minister de Charette in February 1997 to discuss Europe's role in NATO and with Russian foreign minister Primakov concerning Russia's relationship to the expansion of NATO.

The expansion of NATO, and what it represents, is a matter of

---

46. Thatcher, "The West after the Cold War."
47. Ian Davidson, "Dangerous Liaisons," *Financial Times,* January 22, 1997.

critical importance. What is the role of Russia and the newly independent states of the former Soviet Union in European security, as well as in a European Union? The quarrel during the *Cold War*, after all, was with the communist dictatorship but never with the Russian people. Thus, it is vitally important now that plans to expand NATO are well understood in Russia and that Russian objections to expansion are well understood in America and Europe. British foreign affairs analyst Ian Davidson explains why:

> Nato says it has no quarrel with Russia, and that its enlargement is not directed against Russia. But Nato is not some kind of all-purpose talk-shop; it is the most powerful military alliance the world has ever seen. Its expansion eastwards *must* mean a substantial shift in the balance of power with unmistakable military implications.[48]

Whatever the answers, America will only be one of two actors on the stage of the Atlantic community. Europe will be the other. Both must determine sooner rather than later how they wish to relate to each other. Together they must deal with what Ian Davidson has described as "two fundamental needs: to create institutional links between western and eastern Europe, to promote stability and prosperity in the young democracies of the east; and to establish a constructive political relationship with Russia, which will help it make the transition to the modern world."[49] Dealing with these needs will not be easy, as the debate between Henry Kissinger, who favors expansion of NATO, and George F. Kennan, who does not, illustrates. The needs, however, must be dealt with, as both Americans and Europeans recognize.[50]

---

48. Ibid.
49. Ibid.
50. See Henry A. Kissinger, "U.S. Must Embrace the Expansion of NATO," *Los Angeles Times,* January 12, 1997, and George F. Kennan, "A Fateful Error," *New York*

In its relations with Europe, America must make the transition from *Cold War* leadership, where its views and opinions dominated, to a new kind of leadership, where its views are of equal weight with those of its friends. Both America and Europe bring different perspectives, from different historical experience and from a common heritage of western civilization, to bear on issues of mutual interest. For that, no apology is necessary! Common heritage is a strength, not a fault. America and Europe have an obligation to take advantage of those strengths to give the Atlantic community a new raison d'être. As some have described it, the Americans have *the power to do things* and the Europeans have *the power to see things*. The wisdom of combining both historical strengths to create a new Atlantic community, based on *the values of classical liberalism*, should be self-evident. That is good foreign policy and old-fashioned common sense.

The *reconstruction* of Europe is finished. A *new construction* is now under way. Challenges exist aplenty. They exist in the Maastricht Treaty, in Europe's burgeoning welfare states, in the discussions concerning the future of NATO and how Russia will relate to its western neighbors, in the dramatic expansion of financial markets, and in the revolution of communication technology, which is redefining the international marketplace. *The fax revolution* has contributed to more than the liberation of Central and Eastern Europe from communist dictatorship; it has also produced a new class of political, financial, and Internet entrepreneurs whose view of the world is different from those individuals who built the Atlantic community after World War II.

Fifty years have passed, and Germany and Europe have taken a direction that few, if any, statesmen in America and Europe en-

---

*Times*, February 5, 1997. See also Strobe Talbott, "Russia Has Nothing to Fear," *New York Times*, February 18, 1997, and George Melloan, "Russia's Neighbors Worry About 'Yalta II,'" *Wall Street Journal*, February 24, 1997.

visioned in 1947. This direction, as seen half a century later, has produced a resounding success—economically, politically, and militarily: Western Europe has become economically strong and politically stable. It has maintained a defensive alliance that pre-served peace. And its powers of idea and action—as measured in terms of economic and political freedom, and the will to defend both—have contributed in a major way to the downfall of commu-nist dictatorship. But as far as challenges to individual liberty are concerned, it is *deja vu all over again*.[51] The challenges have not disappeared; they have just assumed different forms. Today those forms are symbolized by the debate concerning the future of NATO and by the Maastricht Treaty. Fifty years ago the forms were symbolized by the black market and shortages in what was left of Europe and by the views of A. J. P. Taylor and the Social Demo-cratic Party of Germany.

There is hope in the observation made by Hayek in a speech delivered in Switzerland on April 1, 1947. He commented on what he had learned as a result of his travels during the previous two years, since the end of the war in 1945:

> One of the most instructive observations . . . was that the further one moves to the West and to countries where liberal institutions are still comparatively firm, and people professing liberal convic-tions still comparatively numerous, the less are these people yet prepared . . . to reexamine their own convictions and the more are they inclined to compromise, and to take the accidental his-torical form of a liberal society which they have known as the ul-timate standard. . . . on the other hand . . . in those countries which either had actually experienced a completely totalitarian regime or closely approached it, a few men had through their

---

51. This phrase is attributed to Yogi Berra, a former catcher for the New York Yankees.

experiences gained a clearer conception of the conditions and value of a free society.[52]

The irony in Hayek's observations is that governments in America and in Europe have become skilled practitioners of compromise and cultivators of special interests. They have, as a consequence, built massive welfare states (the European Union may become one as well) that threaten to destroy the very freedom that allowed the creation of expensive labor markets highly regulated for social reasons, of punitive and confiscatory tax policies, and of stifling bureaucracies.

In the welfare states of Europe, not to mention the United States, *the values of classical liberalism* are at risk, just as they were in 1947 but for different reasons. In fact, one could argue that they are at even greater risk because the terror and deprivation of war and destruction are not here to remind those constructing post-1989 *democracy, politics, and liberty* that freedom is not inherited. It is earned! America and Europe have a great deal in common, including common obligations. So I conclude with Edmund Burke, from "Letters on a Regicide Peace" (1796):

> Nothing is so strong a tie of amity between nation and nation as correspondence in law, customs, manners and habits of life. They have more than the force of treaties in themselves. They are obligations written in the heart.

---

52. Archives of the Mont Pelerin Society, Hoover Institution, Stanford University.

*Robert Conquest*

CHAPTER TWO

# On Russia
*Economics and Politics,*
*Heritage and Tradition*

I

Russia looms large on our horizons, an uncomfortable companion on the world scene. It stands weak, in a sense which is troublesome, and strong, in a sense which is even more troublesome, a chaotic and struggling mass and one still with a myriad nuclear warheads. A hundred years ago a Russian poet could write

> You are strong, you are weak
> You are rich, you are poor,
> Mother Russia.

These paradoxes still apply.

In considering Russia today, we need to look at three matters: the main forces and experiences which have formed the country's public consciousness, the main elements of its situation as it is today, and the main perspectives of its future. That future may itself also be seen in terms of three main questions. Will its political system develop favorably? Will its economy be transformed?

Will the country become a peaceful component of the world scene?

As I write, it is only just over five years since Russia was, as it were, cast up bruised and broken on to the shores of the modern world. But understanding Russia in the West has long been vitiated by a number of misconceptions. These came from left and right, but all of them shared one major fault: They believed that Russia was a country or culture that was fully interpretable in terms familiar to Western ways of thought.

When the Soviet system collapsed, there were many in the West who thought that a transition to the obviously preferable, and obviously successful, arrangements of the West—democracy and the market economy—would spring to life in short order. Freedom was a normal human aim, while Economic Man would, it was imagined, swiftly emerge from the bondage in which he had been suffering. But Russian experience, Russian goals, Russian habits of mind had been so different from those of the West that these perspectives proved fallacious, in fact dangerously misleading.

## II

Above all, nations do not escape their history. A hundred years ago, Anton Chekhov wrote of Russia's "heavy, chilling history, savagery, bureaucracy, poverty, and ignorance . . . Russian life weighs upon a Russian like a thousand ton rock." And the century which has meanwhile passed was a yet more atrocious experience.

An earlier writer than Chekhov, Ivan Turgenev, noted that all the liberties of the West were rooted in the Middle Ages and that Russia "had no Middle Ages." This is indeed a crux. Magna Carta was signed in 1215; the Mongol invasion of Russia began within a decade.

Vassaldom to the Mongols thoroughly de-Europeanized the Russian political and civil tradition. But even when, after generations, Russia reemerged, the country lived in an almost permanent state of mobilization as the frontier against the continual menace from the steppe. For hundreds of years the threat was permanent. Moscow was sacked by the Crimean Tatars as late as 1571. As a result, Russia had always to keep what was, by the standards of the time, a huge army on the frontier till winter made the routes impassable to raiders. Unlike the brief campaigns of feudal levies in Western Europe, this military service was permanent and universal. Some sixty-five thousand men (it is estimated) were regularly called up, a very large army by comparison with those raised in periods of crisis in France and Germany, which then had considerably larger populations than Russia: The French army at Crécy, the largest hitherto seen in feudal Europe, was twelve thousand men, and the Germans could not raise as many as twenty thousand to face the great Turkish invasion. The Russian effort was thus a killing one. As the historian Pavel Miliukov writes in *Ocherki Po Istorii Russkoi Kultury* (Saint Petersburg: Mir Bozhil, 1896–1903), "Compelling national need resulted in the creation of an omnipotent State on the most meagre material foundation; this very meagreness constrained it to exert all the energies of its population—and in order to have full control over these energies, it had to be omnipotent."

As Trotsky put it in *The History of the Russian Revolution* (Ann Arbor: University of Michigan Press, 1957), not only Russian "feudalism" but all the old Russian history was marked by this "meagreness": the absence of real cities, the fact that in its attempt to compete with "richer Europe" the Russian state "swallowed up a far greater relative part of the people's wealth than in the West, and thereby not only condemned the people to a twofold poverty, but also weakened the foundations of the possessing classes," whose growth was "forced and regimented." (The periods of swift industrial growth, both under tsarism and in Soviet times, he notes as being, in fact, the result of that very backwardness.) And, of course, effective militarization entailed expansion.

Rigorous centralization was enforced over huge territories. Even when it took a year for an order to reach its recipient, even on very petty matters, the decisions were made in Moscow and later Saint Petersburg. On the other hand, naturally enough, the great distances made it far more difficult for the scattered subjects to bring any influence to bear on the capital or to coordinate complaints into any general movement.

Over the seventeenth and eighteenth centuries, the autocracy in Russia became more and more complete—far more so than the regimes in France and elsewhere of which the term is often used. Second, right into the nineteenth century serfdom became more general and harsher. Third, as Ronald Hingley succinctly puts it (in his *The Russian Mind* [London: Bodley Head, 1977], p. 3), Russia "never possessed a politically influential upper, middle, or any other class; never any powerful corporate body able to exert irresistible pressure on central authority." Fourth, from Peter the Great's time on, Russia sought to modernize, or Europeanize, not as regards political or civil matters but simply in technology— especially military technology (in 1820 Russia had the most advanced artillery industry in Europe).

There is nothing ethnically Russian in any of this. It is and was the product of the political "culture." For example, it was the common observation of foreign observers that while the old merchant cities of Novgorod and Pskov were regarded by the Hanseatic merchants as particularly creditworthy, this trait disappeared on their annexation to Muscovy. The Hanse now forbade all credit to Russians. Cheating became endemic. An Englishman of the time gives as a reason that, unable to rely on the future, the Russians thought only of immediate advantage, a point confirmed by a German observer. Under such a style of autocracy, there was no real security since the state could at any moment take everything away. That is to say, a complete change in economic attitudes was produced by the attitudes of the state. As Sir George Macartney, the British envoy extraordinary to Russia in Catherine the Great's time remarked: "The form of government certainly is and will always be the principal cause of the want of virtue and genius in this country, as making the motive of one and the reward of both depend upon accident and caprice" (see Peter Putnam, ed., *Seven Britons in Imperial Russia, 1698–1812* [Princeton, N.J.: Princeton University Press, 1952]).

Russians developed a culture of reliance on personal relations—informal networks of acquaintances who to this day help out in anything, from providing the food for a party to getting a dentist who can be "paid" by a service done for him by one or other of the network connections. This in some measure accounts for the current avoidance of socioeconomic collapse. All these characteristics marked Russia right up until the 1990s.

## III

From the 1860s until the Bolshevik seizure of power in 1917 came the beginnings of a political and mental evolution. Serfdom was abolished, an educated middle class started to emerge, a jury system came into being and, after 1905, a comparatively primitive parliament which nevertheless contained members of opposition parties.

All this was destroyed by Lenin and the Bolsheviks. But there was one element of these positive developments that survived: the great literature, through which ideas fundamentally at odds with the new totalitarian mind-set remained in the Russian consciousness. The conservative, religious Dostoevsky, the liberal Chekhov, the anarchist Tolstoy, and all the others were annexed, misinterpreted, explained away but were never suppressed.

## IV

In general, the communist era was morally, intellectually, and physically bleak, far beyond earlier Russian experience. Over seventy years all the other social forces were destroyed and an alien totalitarian order implanted, recruiting to itself a dullard bureaucracy and creating wasteful and parasitical economic forms.

It destroyed at least twenty million human lives and created an atmosphere of terror that swept through the rest of the population. It was accompanied by corruption and incompetence on an enormous scale. All the advances made toward constitutionalism and liberty over the last half century of tsarism were destroyed. Russia became the first truly totalitarian state, whose main concern was to make conformism to a vicious and erroneous doctrine the norm.

The communist period was in fact a threefold disaster. It was demographically a tremendous blow to the country, not only were the actual population losses huge but they fell most heavily on the most advanced elements. The intellectual catastrophe was comparable. And the moral distortions were equally crushing.

Even in the socioeconomic sphere the problems arising were not merely a matter of economics proper. The first influential—though at the time secret—analysis came in 1983 from the official sociologist, Tatyana Zaslavskaya, who later summed up:

> The primary reasons for the need for perestroika were not the sluggish economy and the rate of technological development but an underlying mass alienation of working people from significant social goals and values. This social alienation is rooted in the economic system formed in the 1930s, which made state property,

run by a vast bureaucratic apparatus, the dominant form of own-
ership. . . . For 50 years it was said that this was public property
and belonged to everyone, but no way was ever found to make
workers feel they were the co-owners and masters of the factories,
farms, and enterprises. They felt themselves to be cogs in a gi-
gantic machine. (Quoted in *Voices of Glasnost,* by Stephen F.
Cohen [New York: Norton, 1991], p. 122)

This alienation of the working class was accompanied by a general
alienation and, as far as possible, an opting out of the official
society. As Joseph Brodsky put it: "The worst effect of the regime
was that people stopped allowing themselves to think or feel, and
that to build some sort of personal life by deceiving or avoiding
the authorities came to be thought the highest achievable good."

This was the defensive reaction of the older generation. But
once a generation had grown up which was not accustomed to
unrestrained terror and for which the ruling caste was self-evi-
dently nasty and stupid, the regime was lost. Yet it took time.

Broadly speaking, by the mid-1980s, the younger generation's
attitude to the official dogma, and to the system itself, was one of
contempt. Moreover, by this time that section of the intermediate
generation which constituted the junior levels of the state with
which the young were in direct contact had itself lost faith and
become semicynical or, at any rate, those of them who were not
obvious and notorious dullards. When one met Soviet representatives abroad, one could see that they were embarrassed and
ashamed of the lies they had to tell—not just lies but stupid, de-
grading lies.

The disjunction between the system's claims and the reality—
and in particular the disastrous prospects ahead—had become
clear to some Soviet economists and sociologists twenty and more
years ago. In time this penetrated the official research institutes of
the party and state. Then in the 1980s it reached a section of the
party leadership. When Shevardnadze said to Gorbachev in 1984

on the beach at Pitsumi on the Black Sea, "this can't go on," it was a signal that the end was near. In the long run, falsification failed in the face of long-suppressed but still persistent reality.


## V

More broadly, the economy and the ecology had been driven into the ground by the Soviet regime. On that regime lies the responsibility for the abysmal level from which Russia has to raise itself. But a section of the population looks back on the Brezhnev era as one of comparative prosperity. So, in certain respects, it was—at the cost of using up the country's resources.

And Russian citizens' feeling that perestroika, in its initial phase, made things worse is quite correct. The Gorbachev leadership made two main mistakes. First, the antialcohol campaign produced huge fiscal losses, with few (though some) social gains. Second, the old Soviet habit of solving everything by massive investment again emerged and tied up a vast amount of much-needed capital. That, of course, did not work, and now the market economy is in a general way recognized as the only option.

However, the "creation" of a market economy was to a great extent a misleading concept. Market economies have emerged rather than been decreed. Socialist economies were, of course, consciously set up by the state. The problem in Eastern Europe was to create conditions under which a market economy could come into being. Then, conditions being set, would come the emergence of an entrepreneurial or at least market-oriented class. Some Western economists believed that this would happen automatically. That may be so in the long run, but in practice few were prepared for the new economic regime.

There had, indeed, been a fair amount of illegal, but often marginally tolerated, free enterprise and a certain proportion of economic reality in the USSR. Too much and the system would erode, too little and it would explode. By the early eighties, this was already out of hand. As Professor Alain Besançon, the distinguished French expert on Russia, noted, in the early 1980s, for the first time, money was becoming as important as position in securing the perquisites of the trough—which could result in what he prefigured as "a sort of savage capitalism."

This economic network was linked into the state machine, at its various levels, each with its price. In one of Gogol's novels a bureaucrat is accused of accepting bribes above his station. Similarly, under communism, as a recent correspondent put it, "everyone knew what he was eligible to steal." This important element is still in place, concerned not with productive capitalism but with the apparatchik in his new capacity as businessman and looting the state's funds.

As a Moscow sociologist wrote toward the end of the Soviet era, "Decades of destitution has shaped in our people the psychology of poverty and want," with so much competition for every particle of subsistence that the already notorious Russian penchant for preferring general failure to anybody's success—found indeed in many peasant-rooted societies—was much exacerbated. It should be added that this more or less paranoid attitude to profit also affects the Russian view of Western investment.

VI

The collapse of the Soviet Union can be seen as greatly overdue. Not only had the system failed economically, ecologically, and, finally, even in its military purpose, but, just as important, it had lost credibility, incurred contempt from all the thinking—and feeling—elements of the population.

It had lost not its mandate, something it had never had, but its motivation. It was a classic example of Marx's image of an obsolete political order as a boiler in which the pressure built up inexorably. Stalin had created a boiler with unprecedented thick administrative and ideological walls. The regime survived and outlived its term solely for that reason.

To sum up: we see a country which, out of a backward past, had began to evolve toward a civic order over a half century following the emancipation of the serfs in 1861; which had those developments destroyed in 1917; which then suffered for three-quarters of a century from totalitarian-utopian despotism; which inherited an economy and ecology almost in ruins in a social order heavy with the detritus of that past, a political mentality still charged with the never-abreacted negative attitudes of both the totalitarian and the pretotalitarian history. The legacy of socialism was, in Mikhail Gorbachev's phrase, "collective responsibility and individual irresponsibility."

As the leader of the Palestine Communist Party, Joseph Berger, who himself served a long spell in labor camp, put it in *Shipwreck of a Generation* (London: N.p., 1971) p. 266, Russia after Stalin was like a country "devastated by nuclear war." Economically the USSR was unique: an overdeveloped country with too much industry (particularly heavy industry) producing useless or military goods. A similar point could be made about the extravagant, wasteful methods of oil production, compounded by enormous (and ecologically disastrous) leakages through improperly maintained pipelines. Again, roads and building are in a bad state. In fact, an enormous effort simply to retrieve the disasters inherited by the old regime was and is needed: an effort hard to bring the exhausted Russian people to face, especially after so many years of nonproductive effort forced on them—with such meager results that their whole attitude to work became eroded. On the land the old hard-working peasantry has virtually disappeared. In the factories, "they pretend to pay us, we pretend to work" feelings largely prevailed. In shops, offices, and restaurants, the customer or citizen with legitimate wants was treated almost as a pest. The idea of "service" had gone.

Over the last forty years, the physical annihilation of human beings largely ceased. But the destruction of the economy continued, together with the psychological destruction. The poet Fazil Iskander has written that "under a totalitarian regime, it was as if you were forced to live in the same room with a violently insane man" and that such feelings were deep-rooted and hard to overcome.

We have today a Russia whose citizens' minds, apart from those of the very young, have over a long period been twisted out of anything we could regard as normality by a powerful machinery of distortion. Those negative effects, added to those deriving from earlier history, penetrated most of the population. Nevertheless, not only in the educated classes but throughout Russia, positive signs remained. In 1977, Andrei Sakharov was visiting a labor camp area in Mordovia and spoke to one of the guards in charge, who seemed moved by listening to some poems being recited. In his autobiography Sakharov comments: "Maybe I am naive, but when I think of Vanya's face that day, and of similar encounters, I begin to believe that this wretched, downtrodden, corrupt, and drunken people—no longer even a *people* in any real sense of the word—is not yet entirely lost, not yet dead . . . and compassion for others and a thirst for spiritual fulfillment have not yet been utterly extinguished. Will anything come of them? For the nation as a whole, I have no idea, but is that so important? On the personal plane, I am certain that so long as there are people, the sparks will glow."

The Russia which we now face, and which now faces itself, is marked above all not by impersonal forces but by human beings thinking certain thoughts and as a result performing certain actions. Of the Soviet regime, I wrote thirty years ago (and it applies even more to the Russian present):

We must never fail to bear in mind possibilities which seem re-
mote and extravagant at present. On the form of the past decade
in the Soviet Union and the Communist bloc, we can at least say
that it is highly improbable that an easily foreseeable evolution
will take place in the USSR in the next decade or decades. Which-
ever of the various possibilities becomes actual, we may at least be
reasonably sure that a prediction of the Soviet future based on a
cautious and conservative view, and foreseeing easy and evolu-
tionary development without surprises, can be dismissed as almost certain to be badly wrong. The difficulty, if anything, is the
opposite: to envisage for contingency planning a wild enough set
of possibilities to cover, one way or another, what will actually happen.

Even so, a number of us foresaw that in the long run communist arrangements would ruin the country and sooner or later
collapse. But that was an easy prediction compared with assessing
what might happen next. Seeing a steamer heading through dangerous waters with misleading maps, poor steering, a leaky hull,
ill-trained officers, and a drunken, semimutinous crew, one cannot predict its precise fate, but one can predict disaster. So it was
with the USSR for those who had eyes to see. With a dozen life
rafts, banging into each other, on a stormy sea, with various attempts to assemble them in an organized search for dry land,
hampered by lack of agreement on how and where to proceed, we
cannot say what will happen in the short run, though we may note
that their chances are better than if they'd stayed aboard the old
SS.


VII

The trouble with a velvet revolution is that it does not decisively
liquidate the previous unsatisfactory political forces. It is a sad
reflection on Stalinism's degree of success in indoctrination that

a narrow-minded regressive stratum bearing its imprint still exists in Russia, not only in the political sphere but even in the cultural world.

Nor should one forget fear. The older people do not feel at all certain that the police state may not return. Even the erratic plotters of August 1991 had an execution list ready (including Alexander Yakovlev), which would have been the first political executions since the purge of Beria police elite in 1953–1955.

A prominent Russian academic wrote, at the very beginning of the glasnost period, that Stalinism "spread deep roots into the mentality of several generations . . . the fear which it instilled in our minds and souls still shackles people's consciousness and paralyses it." (Academician Likhachev, *Literaturnaiia gazeta*, 9 September 1987.)

As we have said, the older generation, of course, suffers more than the young from the mental distortions of the Soviet years. Equally, the old are (generally speaking) less able to adapt to new circumstances. Those of pensionable age are, in addition, the losers over the inflation and so tend to be antireform and in favor of the not-so-ex-Communists who promise higher pensions. Already, the amount going into pensions, including early retirement deals, is a high proportion of government expenditure.

When communism collapsed, there was the general hope that Western-style "democracy" would save Russia not only as regards internal politics but also in the economy, with the help of—in fact, unavailable—funds from the West, quickly bringing the country up to "American levels of prosperity."

Naturally this was not in the realm of possibility. As for Western subsidies bringing the Russian economy into a modern condition, Germany barely had the resources to undertake the, on the face of it, much easier equivalent for the eighteen million people in the old East German Soviet zone and then only with still unresolved disruption.

Credits moreover are worthless unless the system is changed in a way that ensures their being put to good use. Eighteen billion dollars of credits were given to Poland under the old communist regime; it was all wasted—the West lost the money and the Polish economy remained as bad as ever. But the West, up to a point, had learned the lesson. So the West could not, in this sense, "save" Russia.

But when unlimited Western funds were not forthcoming, the best thing would have been to attract Western investment. This, however, involves Western profits, which come under the same suspicion as other profits. There is now widespread anti-Western feeling on this issue and a commonly heard notion that the West is conspiring to "rob Russia." Western technological investment in Russian oil is widely so regarded in spite of the enormous economic profits seen everywhere in the world where such investment has been made. Even Lenin saw the advantages of attracting foreign investment in a then moribund Soviet economy, saying, in 1920, that it would be of advantage to rent land out to foreign concessions: "Even if we give up half, even three-quarters of the produce, we still stand to gain." (Speech of December 6, 1920, to the Moscow Party Congress.)

Many Western firms have over the past few years sought to invest in the USSR, and others, to find trading partners. There have been successes. But, on the whole, Western interest has waned considerably.

Negotiations and agreements with leading economic or governmental figures were often fruitful and promising. But when it came to the implementation of such agreements, things became more troublesome. At the lower level, the procedures were and are often devoted to fulfilling a mass of regulations and rulings which seem to exist for their own sake. Moreover, inexplicable delays are commonplace. One Western director described his experience as "like walking in glue." Over and above this, contracts are often not fulfilled or are subject to unforeseen revision. And, above all, the absence of a modern fiscal and financial system is a continual obstruction not only to foreigners but also to Soviet economic recovery.

The post-Lenin Communists still do not see this—in spite of the huge economic successes of the oil states. And not only Communists, but a wide range of Russians, take the same narrow view. As we have said, this attitude to profit extends to their fellow citizens as well.

A 1995 poll taken shows that only 5.1 percent of Russians believe that talent and hard work can bring wealth; 44.2 percent said that speculation was a more likely route, and 20.4 percent identified money laundering as a way to get rich. Even those who have become wealthy tend to agree; 18.3 percent of entrepreneurs said that criminal money plays a big role in their lives, and 40 percent of the self-identified new rich said that they had engaged in illegal activities on the way up.

On the positive side, polls have shown that even in Russia the numbers of those saying that reform has been too slow are larger than those saying it has been too fast. Nevertheless, more than a quarter want a return to a planned economy. There is a reason beyond cultural habit for this attitude: A great deal of the current accumulation of wealth is indeed more or less criminal, at least to some degree dependent on criminal connections.

The Russian criminal stratum, dating back four hundred years, was the only social element the Communists failed to penetrate and control (if we except a few special cases—underground religious groups, gypsies, and the clans of the North Caucasus). This stratum reemerged more publicly after the collapse of the regime and was soon operating in its old symbiosis with a section of the apparat. There was indeed greater activity as well as greater visibility. Moreover, new non-Russian gangs arose devoted to minor racketeering and turf wars. One major incentive to small businesses's cooperating with the mafia is that its fees are much lower than the prohibitive high taxes such connections can help them avoid.

In 1992 to mid-1995, forty-five bankers were murdered. Bankers and other businessmen now employ some ten thousand bodyguards in order to have a reasonable chance of staying alive. As ever in such circumstances, inflation and law enforcement were inevitably corrupted. The open proliferation of violent crime is seen by many Russians as the main problem of today.

Then again, the only group experienced in industrial management were the old economic apparatchiks—some ready for change, others less so, others not at all—and none, in any case, more than indirectly subject to market considerations. Insecurity, as against the bureaucracy, the state, the overlapping criminal element, the absence of reliable law, is endemic.

To write of post-Soviet Russia is to examine "rubble," as Solzhenitsyn put it. The collapse of the old structure has left a chaos which has not yet settled into anything like normality. The immediate political outlook is confused, with no clear outcome, a turbulence of conflicting and often self-destructive interests, and a government (and a governmental system) with shaky public legitimization.

The situation in Russia, and in the other postcommunist countries, could not have been one of either instant democracy or instant capitalism. A useful general view might be that in Russia a capitalism has emerged which has been distorted by bureaucracy and interest groups emerging from the remnants of the old system. There are comparisons to be made: Russian "capitalism" resembles the most elitist and state power–driven, crime-ridden South American capitalism, while elsewhere in Eastern Europe—Hungary, say—the stage reached is more like that of Italy before the recent partial collapse of its parasitical politico-economic arrangements. (The Czech Republic is, of course, an exception.)

Those now accumulating money come in several categories:

1. The managerial barons of the old industrial sector (the exemplars of which are also often the local political barons)

2. The representatives of the old criminal class, already linked to a section of the above even in communist times

3. Genuine entrepreneurs and merchants operating under such constraints from elements 1 and 2 that they are usually under pressure to make quick profits rather than healthy investments

After five years, Russian leaders are telling the country, as if it were a new discovery, that it needs a reliable legal system, the rule of law, the enforceability of legal contracts.

## VIII

There are other difficulties of political psychology and culture—and not only on the conservative side. In a speech in 1990 to the Union of Writers in Leningrad, I said that I hoped to see a series of free elections with Sakharovite and Solzhenitsynite parties competing and ceding power peacefully when defeated. One questioner was puzzled: "But if one of them is right, it would be wrong for it to lose power." Habits of mind of major cultures are not changed easily or suddenly. Chekhov said three generations ago that Russia needed to "squeeze out the slave drop by drop."

Even in the late 1980s, one heard, at every level of society, "We want to become a normal country." The old Russian addiction to the sacred empire or the coming Utopia was dying out—even among intellectuals. It is not gone entirely. But the current complaint—that the people are becoming more and more apolitical—

is a sign of that falling off in "enthusiasm" which is necessary in a stable society. It is sometimes urged that the creation of suitable "institutions" in countries evolving into democracy is the central problem and, if correctly solved, will be almost sufficient in itself.

I chanced to read the Russian Constitution while it was still in draft. It was clearly the result of hurried compromises that had not yet been sorted out, but the final version showed little improvement. The idea of checks and balances, which it inherited from American-style constitutional thought, did not work out as foreseen in theory. (As one Russian commentator has pointed out, in Russia the existence of different concentrations of power led, in 1993, not to compromise but to armed conflict.)

Model constitutions have been tried all over the world with at best mixed results. In Russia, the coming into effect of the present constitution has at least provided a set of rules which, though awkward, have been generally obeyed or at least treated as binding by most of the political forces—at any rate for the time being.

One institution not provided for in any formal sense in most democratic countries is a healthy party system. In Russia, there are indeed political groupings, none of them strong enough to take on all the others, but the true political parties necessary to a balanced polity are largely missing. The "parties" within such groups are multifarious and fissiparous. One Russian politician speaking of a proposed "left-center" coalition, commented, "You can't make a tiger out of fifty mice."

A real "lesson" from the West would not be on constitutional forms but on political realities. Ben Pimlott, in his *Labour and the Left in the 1930s,* shows that the Labour Party only ceased to be marginal in 1918 with Arthur Henderson's transformation of party organization from a loose coalition of electoral allies into a body of tightly knit local branches, rigorously based on electoral boundaries, constituencies, boroughs, and wards—and subordinating all other considerations to the electoral aim. In Russia, only the Communist Party has anything resembling such a network, and even that is incomplete. Above all, as the democratic leader Yuri Afanasiev has written, Russia lacks a democratic conservative party.

As to the practical division of power, much of it is in the hands of regional bosses or interests, some of them maintaining a relationship with one or the other national party but in practice operating very much in their own behalf. Some of them even have what amount to their own tariff boundaries, and almost all are only partly amenable to central control. The provinces, in their partial disalignment from the center, themselves greatly differ. In some, the new neo-capitalism with its ostentatious Mercedes culture is important and influential; in others, it has scarcely penetrated. But even where the Marxist aura is absent, most cities are still run by the feudal apparat.

In the countryside, we find the peasantry, now a minority, remnant of those driven from the land or escaping it to the city. Broadly speaking, they were under the control (often politically, too) of a technically superfluous rural management bureaucracy (in some areas somewhat relaxed to a degree of true cooperative farming) and have to cope with the still fairly intractable sale and distribution system.

## IX

One almost universally held view is that a return to the old economic system is impossible—though, of course, impossible is a word to be avoided in speaking of the Russian future. As against the narrow and shallow pressures of obsolete ideas and shortsighted interest groups, the overwhelming priority of any even fairly sensible government in Russia is thus seen as, obviously, to restore the economy, in fact, to make possible an economy of a type viable in modern conditions. But how?

Vaclav Klaus, the prime minister of the Czech Republic, has explained the essentials of some of the problems. As he puts it, reform is bound to be painful: "The systemic transformation is not an exercise in applied economics or applied political science" but a process involving the whole population and destroying "the former political, social and economic equilibrium." To succeed, it must be continually, carefully, and credibly presented to the citizenry. This requires the formation of standard political parties, without which there is no hope for politicians and no "mechanisms" for democratic politics. It involves institutional changes—political, economic, fiscal, and legal—together with changes in habits and customs. None of this can be "masterminded" by any a priori plan. And, he adds, "the costs the people have to bear must be widely shared, otherwise the fragile political support is lost." Nor could the formal institutionalizing of "democracy" or the launching of a "market" form of economy provide the immediate attainment of Western standards.

As the USSR staggered into its crisis, a prominent Moscow liberal wrote, "We cannot go back to Stalin, but we could still become a second-class country—poor, cruel, and cut off from the West." As I write, a certain stasis has set in, which cannot last at its present level. Expert observers differ strongly in their economic and other assessments. At present one can only say that a long-lasting crisis affects the country. A variety of well-informed but incompatible judgments on that future are now being put forward, which may imply that immediate prospects, at least, rest on a knife edge.

After all these negatives, all this gloom, is there anything more to say? Yes. Although Russia has a hard path to recovery and is a mass of archaic and dangerous psychological burdens, that is not the whole story. On the plus side, there are a number of points.

The media are still remarkably free, expressing views critical of the regime and telling facts unpalatable to it, too.

The country has now had five years of political experience—not as good as five hundred but better than nothing. Then, ideology is virtually extinct in even moderately educated circles. On the economic side, political organizations of all types pay at least formal tribute to the market. In the realm of ideas, as we have said, the totalitarian epoch never effectively suppressed the thought of the Russian Enlightenment; its epigones remain in their different ways broad and humanist indictments of the totalist mind-set.

As far as natural resources go, Russia is a rich country. A proper exploitation of its raw materials alone would be enough to ensure prosperity (though at present there is still enormous wastage). Other favorable signs are also often of a negative type. That the country has not experienced total political breakdown is in large part due to a concomitant breakdown of organization and authority, which has left more of a "rubble" than a structure, with each particular grouping hostile to the ambitions of others and thus blocking totalitarian solutions. This is true not only of national politics, insofar as that exists, but also in the sense that the rulers of regions do not obey government orders and have no desire for a forceful rule of any sort from the center. It may be said that Russia is in a state of suspension between a variety of near futures; if *rien dure comme le provisiore* and a tolerable if shifting balance can be struck, this may—or might—lead in the long run to real progress.

It was suggested earlier that the present political apathy of the population weighs against extremism in both internal and external policy. But this presents two dangers: first, of course, that sooner or later an adventurer, supported by only a marginal element of the country, might win power, even if only temporarily, and still do much damage; second, that the apathetic element might itself be swept off its feet by some appealing demagogue. Once more we are in the realm of the imponderable.

A peaceful economic and political evolution faces extreme difficulties. The West and the International Monetary Fund can only do so much. They have so far failed even in that. Cooperation in the world order with Russia will not necessarily be without friction. As we have seen, an important section of the post-Soviet political leadership, especially within the foreign policy establishment, takes a fairly traditional view of Russia's "state interests." These include (for them) concern for Russians in the non-Russian republics—potentially a dangerous subject.

Russia is still powerful militarily and remains a large presence on the world map. Clearly, it must be encouraged to play a peacekeeping role in its capacity as a world power. The actual disintegration of the Russian state would be a disaster—and while nuclear weapons still abound, it would be a danger on a world scale. A truly despotic Russia would be, if not quite as dangerous, still deplorable. But short of that we will, in any case, be faced with a state and nation of major proportions. How are we to deal with it?

First, we must aim to work together with even a tolerably cooperative Russia in containing the various threats to peace around the world. But second, we must above all do everything we can to discourage any Russian imperialist expansionism. This discouragement must include every possible rebuff to imperialist threats or actions and to expansionist factions in Moscow.

It will be seen that difficulties of precise balance or interpretation arise. But incentives to Russia to cooperate on a world scale, with disincentives to its becoming itself part of the problem, are the clear essentials.

## X

As to politics, Moscow's dominant political element can meanwhile be defined in a general way as, in Russian conditions, "centrist." That is, it rejects the more democratic and market-oriented forces on the one hand and the reactionary neo-Communists on the other.

Not that this establishment is united—there are "left" and "right" centrists; moreover, the struggle at the top is, in part, as Paul Goble has pointed out, between several interest groups such as "the military industrial complex versus the oil and gas conglomerate, and the agro-industrial complex versus consumer groups," in each case seeking control of sections of the state and the economy and making money through their "privatization."

The centrist aim is, in effect, in spite of divisions over the spoil, to defend the interests of those who have profited economically and otherwise over the past five years against both the newly and earlier impoverished from below and a possible takeover of power by reformers from above. Thus, they stand for no return to the past or the old state planning system but equally for no move forward to a democratic order and a more competitive economy, relying instead, as the governmental economic adviser Liudmila Pyiskeva has put it, on "a limited democracy with a semi-state, semi-privatised economy . . . anarchic, corrupt, and oligarchic."

That is the main prospect under the present regime and its probable successors. It is opposed by the disunited liberals on the one hand and the also disunited "red-browns" on the other and by the general possibility of a military or other dictatorship.

As to this last, a "legal" coup (or, in other circumstances, faked election results) would probably be accepted, though only with considerable confidential negotiations on local privileges. Such a coup—as with Hitler in "constitutional" Germany—is not excluded (though it is only the institutional parallel that needs be noted at the moment). But a mere "seizure of power," as with Lenin's coup on November 7, 1917 (by no means impossible), seems less plausible—or at least likely to lead to an unpredictably chaotic interlude. Could Russia survive and reemerge? It is like asking can one go over Niagara Falls in a barrel and survive. One can: it has been done.

General Lebed and other contenders for power, even some of those devoted to progress, suggest that a temporary dictatorship, with the suspension of parties and politics for two or three years, might be necessary. This is sometimes called the Pinochet solution; and indeed some dictators, like General Pinochet, have had certain economic successes. But this was in countries where the state was not much involved in the economy, and where the economic structure built up under previous democratic regimes was still basically sound, so that only a little needed to be done. These were, in any case, local, special, small-scale successes; in general, the free market and political liberty go hand in hand. At any rate, when it is necessary to enlist the efforts of the whole people in a complex economic restructuring, why should anyone think that dictatorship will work?

There is a confusion, especially in Russia, between the enforcement of law and dictatorship. It is not the people, or political diversity, which is holding things up. It is a bureaucracy which has got into the habit of not fulfilling contracts, not fulfilling duties. In the democratic countries, contracts are enforced, delinquents fined or dismissed, without any necessity for dictatorship. (When we speak of the rule of law, we mean contract law as well.)

General Lebed's name raises the whole question of military rule. It is argued that the military is by no means united (and, incidentally, that the present state of the Russian forces is so deplorable that the sane elements in the high command, whatever their longer-term hopes, would not support a really dangerous adventure).

In general, when there is talk of the danger of fascism in Russia, we cannot at present envisage anything like the regimes which are usually so described. Tatiana Tolstaya, when asked if fascism could come to Russia, answered that nothing worked in Russia and fascism couldn't either. It is certainly true that Hitler was able to use the efficient mechanism of the established German bureaucratic apparatus and that no such machinery exists in Russia. But this is to say not that a neo- or subtotalitarianism could not come to power, merely that it could not manage to consolidate or justify its rule.

Political upsets in Russia are possible. Even so, reversion to the old economics, let alone the old political system, does seem virtually impossible. One reason is that, except among a stratum of dinosaurs, Marxism is extinct—in the sense that it is simply reported with no more than a sneer in anything resembling intellectual debate, as is even more the case in Eastern Europe (though one philosophy professor at Prague University is said to be a "Marxist"). Yet a peculiar anomaly—there are now voices in Russia who have given up Marx but kept Lenin! For this is the position of the Russian Communists, who combine various nationalist and dictatorial notions in a demagogic and dubious mishmash. They could in the right circumstances take or share power. They could hardly contribute to solving various problems, but meanwhile, they could do much damage. This is particularly so, of course, in the context of the new nationalism.

## XI

The old Russian paranoia persists. Many Russians feel, as we have noted, that foreign investment is somehow designed to rob them.

They have little tradition of mutual benefit, as against a winner and a loser in an exploitative situation.

Not that this is all there is to be said about the matter. Anti-Western moods are common for other reasons, while there is also much in the notion that being a great power is somehow a compensation for a low standard of living. The Russian style of chauvinism—rather like that of the Kaiser's in Germany—is also seen as a way of gaining "respect," as youth gangs say in the West in similar circumstances. The worry about what foreigners will think of Russia goes back a long way and is to be found, in similar form, in Ivan the Terrible's time and in Nicholas the First's. All such factors tend to turn patriotism into its evil twin, chauvinism. The tendency exists in less virulent form over a wide political segment. I have spoken with several of the senior representatives of the idea of Russia as a great power. They are by no means Stalinists or neofascists. Still, the claim to such status certainly appears as a threat to, for example, Ukraine. I always suggest to Russians of that persuasion that Russia's role as a great power should be largely expressed in a concert of powers, like the old Concert of Europe, defending the world against pirate states and containing local outbursts. It seems very much in our interest to accept, encourage, and give fair place to such a Russia. All the same, it must be said that powerful representatives of this trend have been supporting, or at least condoning, Serbia and, more disturbingly, for reasons that make no real sense.

So Russia is still a potentially dangerous power. Not as overwhelmingly dangerous as the USSR was; in those days world problems could not be solved—the USSR either created them or exploited them. Nowadays, there is no longer in Moscow a serious political power devoted to unappeasable hostility to all other political entities, planetwide. The trouble of course is that an even temporarily aggressive Russia could in some circumstances blunder into situations of a very dangerous sort.

Russia is in an exhausted and politically apathetic condition; but though this to some extent paralyzes extreme action, it is also compatible with a desperate acceptance of dictatorship. Again, Russia is in a general way sick of bloodshed—and Russians overwhelmingly opposed the Chechen war, even though the Chechens are the most unpopular minority in Moscow. There is little desire for war against the West or even China. On the other hand, even among the peaceably inclined there is a response to chauvinistic rhetoric, which, however little its dupes intend it, may help lead to a dangerous and aggressive regime.

## XII

There are reasonable prospects of the huge entity that is Russia, after a difficult and wearisome transition, becoming a normal country. There are also prospects of more negative and dangerous futures. This is a crux in world history; we in the West can best contribute to a favorable evolution by giving what aid and encouragement we can to the favorable developments, by neither provoking nor appeasing the darker forces at work, and, above all, by opening our minds to a deeper understanding of Russia's whole historical, psychological, political, and economic identity, rooted in experiences so different from our own.

*Dominique Moïsi*

CHAPTER THREE | # A European Triangle
*France, Germany, and the United Kingdom*

Politics and arithmetic do not always correspond. In simple arithmetic two plus one equals three. In European politics, the outcome of the equation involving Germany, France, and the United Kingdom is less clear: two plus one may result in less than two. In fact, it may well be argued that, in the past fifty years, a triangle never existed between Germany, France and the United Kingdom. There was, and still is, an emotional marriage of reason between France and Germany. The British were at best perceived as a flirt, a fiancé, not a legitimate member of the couple. The British government may well seem to advocate polygamy as a better formula than "political marriage"; the French and the Germans seem to be saying, like Lady Di in a celebrated interview, that, in a couple, "three is a crowd." To understand this structural imbalance, one must integrate two decisive factors: Europe and the United States. Without their respective attachments to the European ideal, France and Germany could not have been so close. And, by contrast, it is Europe and not the Channel that separates the United Kingdom from France and Germany. Now that the cold war is over, the Soviet Union no longer constitutes the unifying threat that bound the three countries together. But the United States and the institution that symbolizes its presence in Europe (i.e., NATO) are as much limits to division as permanent sources of frustration or even tensions among the three countries of the second triangle. If one cannot understand the relationship between France, Germany, and the United Kingdom without Europe and the United States, their respective perceptions of their national identities as much as the comparative evolution of their "clout" are key elements of the second triangle.

France belongs to an elite group of nations that still believes, rightly or wrongly, not only that the world matters to them but that they matter to the world. For these nations, international identity is an essential part of national identity; they can and must make a difference on the international scene. Germany, by contrast, is selective over the issues on which it adopts a high international profile. It is still torn between the comfort of hiding behind its past and the temptation to broadcast its unrivaled economic clout in Europe. Whereas for France Europe is an attempt to pursue a policy of greatness through other means, a desperate search to prolong a past of influence and glory, for Germany it is exactly the reverse. Europe, together with the Atlantic alliance, has been the radical means to break away from one's immediate past and twelve years of barbarism.

As for the British—though, like the French, they still seem willing to take military action as the essence of nationhood, if not manhood, its *ultima ratio*—they appear to define their international identity increasingly in economic terms. They are also focusing obsessively on their relationship with Europe and thus are less keen than in the past to fly the Union Jack in other parts of the world. If the French see Europe as an extension of their national identity, if the Germans hide their identity behind Europe, the British find it difficult to reconcile their identity with their belonging to Europe. In the last twenty-five years, every incoming

French government without exception has tried to bring the British into the core group of Europe. Paris felt that the United Kingdom would contribute to a healthier and more secure Franco-German relationship because, in the long run, Europe would be better off if it did not depend exclusively on the vitality of the Franco-German alliance. This approach was largely based on traditional considerations about the balance of power in Europe. Paris and London would be better able to balance Bonn, not to mention Berlin, than Paris alone. Yet by the end of the day all these approaches proved unsuccessful, essentially because of the British attitude. There is, quite simply, no alternative to the bilateral approach between France and Germany if one wants to make true progress toward the objective, an ever-closer European Union.

## A "European Germany"

Since 1990, Germany has been united and aware of its new centrality in Europe. It has stopped behaving as an economic giant and a political dwarf, though it has not yet fully overcome its tendency to believe that good intentions matter more than good deeds.It is slowly learning to take the political initiative and to "transcend" the taboo of military intervention. But it is doing so slowly. The "German question" has not been fully answered by the reunification of 1990. Fitting this colossus into the European environment remains a problem. The European Monetary Union (EMU) is not only an economic project but also a means to overcome what some perceive as the monetary hegemony of the German Bundesbank.[1] For Chancellor Helmut Kohl, as well as for his predecessors, European integration and Atlantic ties are still the

---

1. Dominique Moïsi and Michael Mertes, "Europe's Map, Compass and Horizon," *Foreign Affairs*, January/February 1995.

central elements of Germany's *raison d'état* and the cosmopolitan mind-set of its postwar generation; they are also the means with which to contribute to the building of international confidence. United Germany needs its neighbors and partners' confidence to prevent them from envisaging coalitions to balance and contain its demographic, economic, and political clout. Seen from Bonn, Germany's fear of coalitions is not paranoia as long as European leaders still believe in nineteenth-century-style balance-of-power politics. It is in this sense that Chancellor Kohl sometimes warns his visitors that Europe is now confronted with a hard choice: the completion of the EMU or war. Obsessed by memories of the past, when, as a young man, he dug corpses out of the bombed ruins of destroyed German cities, the chancellor puts his entire political weight into a project, which, *faute de mieux*, has been equated with the cause of Europe.

For Kohl, the failure of the EMU would challenge the entire European dynamic and allow the forces of nationalism, which have proven so destabilizing in the eastern part of Europe, to return to haunt the western part of the continent as well. He sometimes considers himself as the last barrier against the return of the poison of nationalism. His message to his European partners could be summarized in one formula: Seize the opportunity to move toward European unification while it is available (i.e., when "*I am still in control as chancellor of the most powerful country in Europe*"). Kohl presents Germany in Europe the way the United States presents itself to the world, as a "benevolent giant." Some Europeans, especially in Britain, may argue that Germany hides its national ambition "under Europe's name." For them, the only remaining major issue for the European Union is its eastward enlargement; a closer union would only help Germany achieve the European hegemony for which it reached in two world wars. In terms of influence, however, Germany—surrounded by countries that regard Bonn (or Berlin) as the center of gravity—would probably be the only major beneficiary of a mainly eastward enlargement. The Germans answer such suspicions by saying that the more member states the European Union has the smaller each share of the power pie becomes. Germany's political class is also prepared to give up some of the sovereignty it has acquired through unification, believing almost unanimously that it is the only way to escape the foreign policy traps of the past.

One cannot escape the feeling that Germany, given its federal system, is also more in tune with the likely evolution of the European continent than France. A country where the nation ended up creating the state can adjust itself more easily to the requirements of the modern world than a country like France, which lived through the reverse experience, whereby the state created the nation by struggling against all forms of regionalism and particularism. In a world where the state has become too small for the big problems and too big for the small problems, the German model is probably more suitable than the French one. But what is the meaning of such an adaptation if the future of the new Europe has little to do with the federalist dream of its founding father and if, in political terms at least, the upholders of a supranational Europe are fighting a losing battle with the rising forces of an intergovernmental vision of our future continent? In this context, the Germans will have to confront their destiny increasingly in terms of the nation-state, however anachronistic these words may sound on the eve of the twenty-first century. It is therefore necessary for the Germans to assess their new role and their new weight as a unified nation. Can the new Germany, whose capital is about to move to Berlin, be a mere continuation of the modest, provincial, guilt-ridden state whose capital was Bonn? In a deep sense, if one compares, for example, the weight of the extreme right of the Republicans in Germany with the weight of the extreme right of Le Pen's National Front in France, it seems obvious that the "vaccination" impact of the Nazi years on Germany still works. It may change if unemployment continues to grow in Germany, but, as things stand today, the extreme right is much less important in Germany than in France. When it comes to foreign policy, the German national interests, as summarized by the noted German historian Michaël Stürmer, are still expressed around three wishes: to eat well, to sleep quietly, and never to be alone.[2] From that point of view, Germany's dreams are much closer to those of the Swiss than to those of their closest friends and partners, the French. Public opinion is no more interested in foreign policy issues than it was before unification. The only two questions that create the beginnings of an interest are linked to the controversy over the participation of German soldiers in peacekeeping operations within the United Nations forces or, more fundamentally, the debate on the future of the European Monetary Union.

Germany may be, according to the title of Hans Peter Schwartz's latest book, *The Central Power in Europe*,[3] but the German dilemma today has little to do with the dilemma faced by the Germans in the era of Willhem the Second at the time of Bismarck's departure. A new world is about to start, with a new Germany at its center; but democracy is well and firmly grounded, and the aggressive nationalism of yesterday no longer exists as an active force. Like France, Germany knows no threat at its border and no longer has enemies. Because of its geography, its culture, and its history, Germany is more preoccupied than France by the future evolution of Central and Eastern Europe and Russia. More than anyone in the West, the Germans are keen to strike a balance between their desire to satisfy their Central European neighbors (the Poles in particular) with their integration into a new NATO

---

2. Michaël Stürmer, "1989. Les conséquences pour l'Allemagne," *Politique étrangère*, automne 1996.

3. Hans Peter Schwartz, *Die Zentralmatch Europas. Deutchlands Rückkehn auf die Weltbühne* (Berlin: Siedler Verlag, 1994).

and a new European Union and their will to reassure Russia of their positive intentions. The depth of the emotional links between Chancellor Kohl and President Boris Yeltsin can only reinforce such a policy. In fact, the word that characterizes the definition of Germans' national interest and the formulation of their foreign policy priorities, despite a drastically changed international context, is *continuity*. More than ever, the United States continues to be the ultimate guarantor, life insurance, "gentle, benevolent" superpower, and protector of the German new international and national identity. In 1997, no less than in 1963, the Germans would (as at the time of the Elysée Treaty) not do anything to endanger the quality of their relations with the United States. Such an attitude, which constitutes a guarantee of stability and continuity for Europe as a whole, represents at the same time a drastic limitation to the French ambition to challenge the American security domination and the French ambition to constitute a truly autonomous European security entity.

Although the German chancellor may have silenced German criticism of the resumption by France of its nuclear testing in 1995, and although the Germans may welcome the process of rapprochement between France and NATO, they may resent, like the French or the British, the sometimes "bureaucratic arrogance" of the American diplomacy from Dayton to the treatment of Cuba. Yet if forced to choose between the Americans and the French, today like yesterday, when it comes to security and "high politics," the Germans may not hesitate, despite the strength of their European convictions, to turn toward Washington.

At the same time the Germans will, with the same clarity, always choose Paris over London when it comes to European issues. Seen from Bonn or Berlin, the British are perceived, with growing irritation, as a lost cause, an irritation that can only be compared with British feelings toward the Germans. The incapacity of the British establishment—once incarnated by Mrs. Thatcher—to transcend historical prejudices, or what the Germans would describe as an anachronistic form of paranoia, can, of course, only be resented by the Germans. But, ultimately, what the British may think or say about the Germans— even in its most unsavory, jingoistic form, in the world of soccer, for example—is less important in the eyes of the German establishment than the British vision of Europe. Whereas the Germans try—sometimes heroically—to think in postmodern nation-state terms, the British more than ever cling to the insuperable concept of the nation-state, the alpha and omega of political reality.

Germany may find it difficult to define its new international role within the new Europe. It may be confronted now with the challenge of globalization and unification as well as rising unemployment and a slowly aging chancellor, whose popularity is inevitably facing a process of erosion. It may suddenly find its model less successful than in the past. Yet it would be wrong to consider the present Franco-German evolution as a process of competitive decadence. Whatever its difficulties, tensions, disillusionments, the Federal Republic of Germany, unified around the challenge of its unification, confronts the future with a combination of activism and determination that places it closer to the United States than France, if not in terms of results, at least in terms of spirit and mind-set.

## An Ambivalent France, between Europe and Itself

It is a paradox of sorts that the most ambitious of the three key actors of our European triangle, France, may be the most gloomy about itself, the most uncertain, and the one that faces the greatest adaptation challenges. To describe France as the sick man of Europe may be an exaggeration, but it corresponds to the perception of its elites, if not its public opinion, and as such constitutes an important consideration.

With unemployment continuing at a postwar high, the mood in France is gloomy. The French are disillusioned with President Jacques Chirac, the man they elected more than fifteen months ago. And they expect little from the parliamentary elections of 1998.

*Morosité* has become the code word summarizing the state of mind of the French. Could France, once a driving force in Europe, now be the sick man of Europe, torn by self-doubt, poor economic performance, and fear of the future?

Both Germany and the United Kingdom are suffering the same malaise that affects most of Western Europe: adjusting to globalization, which draws powers away from national bodies and forces reductions in public spending. But that crisis affects France more because there is more state in France and because France has identified its future with the European project. Power in France is excessively centralized in the executive, the higher civil service is dangerously politicized, and scandals are still exploding in the absence of clear rules for financing political parties. The state needs to be reinvented on a more modest and honest basis. Can it be done, given the incestuous relationships among the political, administrative, and business elites? It is unlikely that such a homogeneous group could make the necessary break with conformity and conservatism.

Some observers believe there may be an "Italianization" of the French political system, in which the main parties collapse like a house of cards and give birth to a new republic. But that is unlikely: the French state is more powerful than Italy's, and French society is less dynamic, less willing to take risks than its Italian counterpart. Yet the likely continuation of *morosité* will have an impact that goes well beyond France—one that may constitute one of the biggest challenges to the completion of the process of creating a European Union.

Members of the pro-European majority in the French parliament appear to discuss the single currency with the resignation of early Christians about to die for their faith in ancient Rome: "We will remain faithful to the Maastricht, but we will be wiped out in the next elections." In such a climate, it is hard to believe that the timetable and objectives of economic and monetary union will be acheived if growth does not pick up—whatever officials say.

The contrast between the downbeat mood of young French people and the optimism of young urban Poles, for example, illustrates the crisis of the European Union. The young French (inside the union) feel gloomy and fear for the future; the young Poles (outside the union) are full of hopes for the future.

Instead of being perceived as a goal or—even less ambitiously—as a solution, the European Union is seen as either the problem or as an irrelevant answer to the daily preoccupations of the French: unemployment and insecurity. In a contradictory manner, the European Union is seen as being both too intrusive in a bureaucratic sense and too impotent on the international stage. From the diktats of Brussels to the failure of Europe in Bosnia, the European project is losing its allure and purpose for France. The growing discontent is shrewdly exploited by Jean-Marie Le Pen's extreme right.

The Germans are witnessing events in France with a mixture of bewilderment and anxiety over their potential impact on the timetable for the EMU. Having lost his old friend and ally François Mitterrand, Helmut Kohl does not feel reassured by the new French leadership. Jacques Chirac's dedication to the cause of Europe is seen as less emotional and less deep than his predecessor's.

As the gloom deepens in France, it is hoped that the French state of mind will not strengthen the Euroskeptics in the United

Kingdom. It would be an ironic turn of events when the Labour Party has just come to power, bringing a new and more positive approach to Europe. Europe cannot be fully unified without the United Kingdom. But without a secure, convinced, and firm French presence, the entire European Union project would be placed in jeopardy.

## France and NATO, between Rapprochement and Misunderstandings

When he came to power in 1995, President Chirac, like his predecessor, was convinced that only Europe could justify the French ambition to play a role in the world. He too searched for a synthesis between the German view of Europe (integrationism) and the British insistence on the sovereignty of national governments. The need for such a compromise was of course partly the result of domestic politics and the desire to reconcile France's pro- and anti-Maastricht camps. Yet it went much beyond, largely because the French felt closer to the British on security matters and closer to the Germans on socioeconomic and political ones. As things stand in 1997, two years after President Chirac's ascent to power, Franco-German relations, despite serious difficulties on both sides, are more central than ever, at least in the eyes of the French, whereas the British seem to have once more succeeded in their process of self-isolation from Europe. The somewhat bumpy rapprochement between France and NATO could not by itself alter the course of Franco-British relations, which depend above all on the status of British-European relations.

The fall of the Berlin Wall, the disappearance of the Soviet Union, and the end of the cold war and the Yalta order may have presented France with a tougher challenge of adaptation than any other Western country. Despite the fact that it consistently condemned and rejected the cold war division of Europe, France found the old order extremely comfortable. Germany was divided, alliances were stable, and the protection of the United States and its reassuring presence in Europe quasi-autonomous, notwithstanding the sometimes erratic character of French diplomacy. The post–cold war order could only prove immediately less comfortable for a country who could no longer hide, behind the screen of the superpower rivalry, the gap between its ambitions and its means, its words and its deeds. The first and most immediate challenge of adaptation came on security matters. The French decision of 1966 to leave the integrated military body of NATO looked more and more anachronistic, and France, having long since exhausted its diplomatic merits, had been confronted since the mid-1980s at least with its cost and the self-isolating consequences of being outside the forum where the main decisions to adapt the alliance were taken. Animated by a strong desire to build up an autonomous European security entity, France under Jacques Chirac (a Gaullist president was probably neutral for such a change) came to the conclusion that in order to have more Europe tomorrow in the field of security, more NATO today was an absolute must. To influence its European partners, France had to come closer to them (i.e., to be present at the *re-creation* of NATO to use a formula more in tune with French intentions than the word *reintegration*). It remains to be seen whether France proved too greedy or overconfident in asking too big a price (i.e., a European in charge of the Southern command) in exchange for its full return into the NATO family.

For France, beyond the question of its own position within NATO, the organization itself has to be deeply adjusted, if not reinvented, to survive. For France, the most important element of this adaptation process is the creation within NATO (a remarkable departure from the initial French position) of a European identity pillar. This project is an element of a much larger vision centered on the need to establish a new European architecture at the level of the entire continent, including Russia, and allowing the former members of the Warsaw Pact to become members of Western institutions, be it the European Union or NATO. The lessons of the war in the former Yugoslavia constituted a sobering challenge, proving beyond doubt the limits of the existing conflict prevention and conflict-solving mechanisms. The Yugoslavia quagmire proved the limits of the United Nations formula, and the inadequacy of the common foreign and security mechanisms of the European Union, and reinforced in particular the marginalization of the Western European Union. By the end of the day only NATO (i.e., the United States) truly made a difference. Such a conclusion could only reinforce the French in their conviction that, at least in a foreseeable future, there was no pure European alternative to U.S. participation in the defense of Europe. Such were the lessons of the White Book of defense, issued when François Mitterrand was still president, under the prime ministership of Edouard Balladur. The conclusion of the war in Bosnia only confirmed the French in this vision. Ironically, the disappearance of the Soviet threat over Europe, and the war in Chechenya demonstrating the extent of the decomposition and moral crisis of the Russian army, far from marginalizing the significance of NATO, reinforced its centrality, not only in the eyes of the Central and Eastern European countries that are candidates for NATO's enlargement but also in those of the traditional members of NATO. Confronted with the disappearance of a clear and well-defined threat, and its replacement with a multiplicity of undefined risks, NATO could only appear—for lack of a better alternative—as the most efficient military organization in terms of procedures, command structures, and equipment. On the eve of the twenty-first century, which France perceives as being potentially characterized by great instability with the possible emergence of new regional nuclear powers, nothing will stabilize the European continent more than the maintenance of a permanent, stable, and well-functioning Euratlantic link.

This background helps understand the security priorities of France under Jacques Chirac, which are characterized by an attempt to reconcile a European project with the ambition of a new transatlantic partnership. In essence, these two goals are complementary and indissociable. In practice, their compatibility proved less evident, largely because of the implementation tactics used by France. The three dimensions of the security "revolution" initiated by President Chirac—abandoning compulsory military service, revising the nuclear strategy, and restructuring the defense industry—have a European and, one could even say, a trilateral dimension (i.e., involving France, Great Britain, and Germany).

The choice of a professionnal army brings France closer to the British model and draws on the lessons from the gulf war, where France was only able to contribute one-third of the British component. France's ability to project its forces outside its territory in conjunction with its allies is seen in Paris as a plus for Europe and NATO. The Germans may have expressed irritation, even resentment, at the way the French decision to abandon conscription was announced. But Jacques Chirac had warned Chancellor Kohl of his decision months before it was publicly revealed. If the German defense ministry was caught by surprise, it was not for Paris a Franco-German problem but a German bureaucratic one.

The French decision to resume nuclear testing in the South Pacific may also have confused France's allies and partners as to the future role nuclear weapons would play in French strategic thinking. Chirac resumed nuclear testing not so much to distinguish himself from his predecessor but in the belief that it was necessary if France were to maintain the security, credibility, and reliability of its nuclear arsenal. The aim of the tests was, at least officially, to validate France's ability to produce so-called robust weapons that retain their capability over a long period and to perfect simulation techniques that will make future testing unnecessary. Such arguments could not convince the world. What the French authorities failed to perceive was the impact of the end of the cold war on international and even French public attitudes.

Without the cold war, nuclear weapons seem more dangerous than any threat they could fight off. In terms of public opinion, Chirac's proposal to move toward the Europeanization of the French nuclear deterrent missed an essential point. Europeans, and Germans in particular, do not want to be under the protection of the French bomb or any bomb; they want, above all, to be protected from the bomb. If the nuclear crisis had, in the short run, reinforced the diplomatic and political links between Bonn and Paris, thanks to Chancellor Kohl's remarkable understanding of the French position, the same could not be said of the relations between the two societies. German public opinion saw in the French decision a confirmation of France's arrogance, while French political and administrative elites probably perceived the Germans' public attitude as further proof of German irresponsibility.

In fact, the nuclear factor at first further isolated France from Europe in that the resumption of nuclear testing is perceived as further proof of French arrogance. But lately it has translated into a remarkable deepening of Franco-British cooperation, which had already manifested itself in the conventional field in Bosnia. It has also allowed the opening of the dialogue between France and Germany on a subject that was once taboo: the still rather abstract concept of "concerted deterrence" between the two countries. France is attempting to "Europeanize" its nuclear weapons at a time when the Germans are transcending their refusal to include the nuclear component within the Franco-German dialogue.

The third pillar of the radical French security reform, the reorganization of the French armament industry, is, even more than the other two, a necessary prelude to a European recomposition of the industrial countryside. It is too early, at the time of writing, to know whether the recomposition, based on a triangular game, will work positively for France. Can France rely on its traditional strong political links with its neighbor Germany? Increasingly, German commercial interests are aligned with Great Britain, as witness the Anglo-German alliance between British Aerospace and Daimler Benz Aerospace on restructuring Airbus. In this context, can France still afford to adopt what is perceived in the rest of Europe as a nationalistic, if not chauvinistic, line? France's nationalism has been on display in the first attempt by the French government to privatize Thomson-CSF, the key European defense electronics group; Paris welcomed non-French groups only as subordinates. Seen from France, the French should be in charge because they have the biggest defense business. Seen from London, however, that is less evident since France's companies are neither the most profitable nor the most valuable. The result of this defence reorganization will be decisive not only for France but for Europe. What is at stake is the Europeans' ability to exist in the field of defense electronics in particular and to resist the growing competition of the United States in general.

In this case, either the triangle will work successfully or Europe will cease to exist as an independent actor in a globalized world. The British as much as the French or the Germans may perceive this reality, but they do not seem to derive the "right" political consequences from this industrial challenge. As perceived from Paris or Bonn, the British attitude toward Europe is more distant and aloof than ever, and rightly or wrongly, neither the French nor the Germans expect a radical change to occur with Labour's coming to power in Great Britain.

# Great Britain:
# The Charm and Limits of Splendid Isolation

Nothing defeats more than victory. Since 1945, the British have had constant difficulties digesting their remarkable victory in World War II, which confirmed them in their uniqueness, if not in the inherent superiority of British elites. In fact, one deep cultural reason the convergence of interests beetween the French and the British has failed to bring them closer together may be due to their respective elites. The political and administrative elites of Great Britain and France share a similar kind of statist and historical arrogance, which perhaps makes them too similar to live together.

For more than half a century, British foreign policy was based on a combination of realism and nostalgia. The United States was the key superpower, the only one sustaining a world order compatible with U.S. interests. If sometimes British interests were not identical with those of the United States, Great Britain could accept, as during the Suez crisis, "a quiet humiliation," to quote Michael Howard.[4] Also the British were certainly not Greeks to the American Romans and had in every field much less to contribute than the Americans.

Great Britain, like France, thinks of itself as a great nation attached to its identity and cultural tradition. It is not only a leading figure in the security of Europe but has global interests. London shares with Paris the status of being a permanent member of the United Nations Security Council and of being a nuclear power. Great Britain, like France and Germany, is among the world's leading trading nations and investors. In economic terms, Great Brit-

---

4. Michael Howard, "Reflexions on British Security Policy," *International Affairs* 4, no. 71 (1995).

ain is becoming more integrated in Europe. French companies are running trains and supplying water in Britain. British companies are running telephone services and airlines in France. In fact, one could say that the divide in England is not between conservatives and Labour but between the political and administrative elite and the United Kingdom's economic and financial interests. It is as if Downing Street and the City of London were on different planets.

The politicians are fighting a desperate battle to protect what they see as the United Kingdom's national turf. They still think in terms of regional balance of power and, in the footsteps of Margaret Thatcher, agonize over the best way to balance Germany in Europe now than the Soviet threat has gone and has not (yet) been replaced by a Russian one. The City thinks in term of global competition and sees the importance of regional cooperation. It looks at the balance of power in global terms, wondering how Europe can best balance Asia and America.

It remains to be said that British public opinion continues to perceive Europe as foreign, neither understanding nor trusting it. In fact, the very strength of the Franco-German couple contributes to a British perception that the European Union is not theirs. This leads to greater alienation and further uncooperative behavior, as observed by Robert Cooper, presently minister of the British Embassy in Bonn and a most sophisticated British diplomat.[5]

The more the Euroskeptics portray Germany as aggressive, the more determined German chancellor Kohl becomes to integrate Germany thoroughly into Europe and the more threatening it seems to people in Britain. Britain's continuing obsession with Germany is one of the key factors explaining its relations with Europe. The relations between the two countries are bad, but the

---

5. Richard Cooper, speech at the British Bavarian Seminar, Holenkammer, Germany, 24 July 1996.

Germans care much less about the British, and their press with few exceptions is much more restrained and wise. Around the time of the last European football championship, a certain British tabloid went too far. Why are the British prisoners of the past when it comes to Germany? Is it nostalgia for their own past grandeur? Do they compensate for their sense of relative decline, their perception of the growing centrality and importance of Germany in the new Europe, with a sense of moral superiority derived from the past? The German economy, the German currency may be stronger today, but, say the British, we were "greater" and on the right side of history yesterday, a moral confidence that the French, as a result of their defeat of 1940 and the Vichy regime, cannot enjoy.

The British recognize that modern, democratic Germany is different from the Germany that existed in the first half of the century; yet this recognition is not enough. Euroskeptics in Britain tend to see the European Union as being the result of a German organization, if not a German plot. They see Germany as overregulated and fear the social regulation model, which they associate with Germany even more than with France. They see the EMU too as essentially a German plan.

Confronted with the German, if not the French, drive toward integration, the British propose more cooperation. They see no alternative to the nation-state, the only basis, according to them, for the practice of democracy and the preservation of liberty. The British may cherish an independence, a sovereignty, which no longer exists in the modern world. But the more impotent European institutions appear in the field of security and foreign policy, the more incapable Europe will be of finding solutions to the problems of unemployment and immigration and the more the British vision of Europe will by default attract a greater number of Europeans outside Great Britain. Europe's dilemma can be summarized as follows: Will Great Britain be Europeanized or will the

British view of Europe regain ground as the objectives of Maastricht are progressively lost? The answer to this fundamental question is more open than it seems.

## Conclusion

As long as the gap between the economic and political world remains as large as it is today in Great Britain, France will have no choice but to stick, *faute de mieux*, to working bilaterally with Germany on European integration. Whatever the limits and strains in the relationship between Paris and Bonn, if the British threaten a stalemate at the intergovernmental conference, the French will have only one choice: to resort to a Franco-German initiative to relaunch the dynamic of Europe. Seductive though the trilateral approach may be, there is no alternative to a bilateral approach if France and Germany want to progress toward an ever closer European Union. In any case Paris and Bonn bank on the fact that the well-known pragmatism of the British will force them—sooner or later—to join a process they cannot afford to be excluded from, politically or economically. But that vision is of course based on optimistic scenarios for the future of the European Union.

*Ludger Kühnhardt*

CHAPTER FOUR

# On Germany, Turkey, and the United States

## Changing Geopolitical Parameters

With the end of the cold war, the strategic landscape has begun to change. The East-West divide, symbolized by the Berlin Wall, has not been replaced by new, clear, strategic parameters. Restructuring, consolidating, and stabilizing are the approaches of Western governments aimed at giving a new face to the old world. The concern for new developments beyond the traditional sphere of the East-West divide remains marginal. Yet the world is heading quickly toward new parameters with strategic implications and challenges. To keep pace, Western institutions are forced to run faster than the history that is unraveling in front of everyone's eyes. The political transcription of this physical law of motion remains difficult and is dealt with in an hesitating manner. The challenges are not being made easier by the fact that history has not only moved into a faster gear but is also changing direction. It is no longer sufficient to look only to the East in order to define the role of the West. The South has started to knock at the doors and challenges the West to reflect on new challenges for stability and security.

The future of the Mediterranean Sea and the Middle East, the developments in the Transcaucasian republics and Central Asia, the role of political Islam and reemerging Russian imperialism, the future relationship between Russia and China and between the Arab world and the West are only a few of the new parameters that must be incorporated into any future-oriented strategic thinking. In terms of subjects rather than regions and countries, the list of new parameters must include demographic developments and ethnic strife, politics of oil and water, proliferation of weapon systems, and the threat of economic and political chaos at the doorsteps of NATO and the European Union.

To read this list and view the map inevitably brings Turkey into view. In fact, Turkey has become pivotal in a region that is going through turmoil to get from one stage of stability to another. Where Turkey will go and how Turkey will perceive the new constellations has become an important, if not critical, question for any Western strategy of the twenty-first century. The role of Turkey is bound to the West on the basis of Turkey's membership in NATO. The United States has committed itself to maintain security in and for Turkey. Although more than two million Turks live in Western Europe, the European Union has been hesitant to define Turkey's role in Europe. Germany is considered to be a "partner in leadership" on this subject, but it has yet to deliver. Turkey's own recent ambitions, potential, and development have irritated its Western partners and require clarification. The United States, Germany, and Turkey form a triangle that will remain highly relevant and important for the shaping of a stable twenty-first century.

# Turkey: Bridge or Barrier?

For more than half a century, Turkey's standing and role was clear. Kemal Ataturk, the founder of modern Turkey as a laical republic, in 1923 gave his countrymen a new sense of direction after the fall of the Ottoman Empire. Turkey was developing a liberal, modernizing Islam and played a critical role in containing the Soviet Union. With the fall of the Soviet Union, Turkey and its neighbors began reconsidering Turkey's place in the region and in the world. The Turkish people in turn began reconsidering the role of Islam in Turkish society and the relationship of their country to the West. Was Turkey to become "bridge or barrier?"[1] Was Turkey rediscovering its past rather than forging a common Western future? And was the West becoming increasingly uncertain and divided as to how to see Turkey, with the United States favoring a strategic approach while Western Europe—especially the Germans—concentrated on human rights violations and the Kurdish question?

As the century is about to turn, it is important to reexamine the triangle of Turkey, Germany, and United States. From an American or Western European perspective, the first question is how Turkey is perceived by its Western partners: How is Turkey developing internally and what will be the consequences for its international role? The second question deals with implications and recommendations for Western policy toward Turkey: How should the United States and Germany develop their relationship and partnership with Turkey in light of Turkey's role and potential?

---

1. Ian O. Lesser, *Bridge or Barrier? Turkey and the West after the Cold War* (Santa Monica, Calif.: Rand Corporation, 1992).

# Turkey: Old Ways and New Approaches

In the emerging post–cold war world, Turkey appears to have increased its power and broadened its options dramatically. At the
first summit meeting of the Turkish republics in October 1992,
President Turgut Özal, the key figure of Turkish politics during
the 1980s, promised that the next century would be a "Turkish
century."[2] Özal, who died in office in 1993, was not only referring
to the rediscovery of pan-Turkic ties residing deep in Central Asia
but to a powerful Turkey with variable postures in all directions,
based on domestic political stability and economic prosperity. In
short, President Özal defined his country as the dominant emerging regional power, short of being hegemonic but clearly stronger
than during any period since the fall of the Ottoman Empire.[3]

In the vast region between the Adriatic coast and the Chinese
border, between North Africa and the Middle East, Turkey
adopted a completely new profile as outlined below:

1. With the breakdown of the Soviet empire, Turkey's strategic importance increased not only relative to Russia but
   also as a pillar of stability and magnet for the newly independent countries; it fills the geopolitical vacuum and its
   ambition to be a key actor in a new "great game."

---

2. See also Heinz Kramer, "Die Türkei zwischen Europa, Asien und dem
Nahen Osten—eine aufstrebende Regionalmacht?" *Südosteuropa Mitteilungen* 32,
no. 1 (1992): 129; Eric Rouleau, "The Challenges to Turkey," *Foreign Affairs*, No-
vember/December 1993, p.110; Faruk Sen, "Die Türkei als Ordnungsmacht," in
Günther Wagenlehner, ed., *Konflikte, Konfliktlösung und Friedenssicherung in Süd-
osteuropa*, München: Südosteuropa-Gesellschaft, 1994), p. 130.
3. For Turkey's history, see Stanford and Ezel Shaw, *History of the Ottoman
Empire and Modern Turkey*, 2 vols. (Cambridge: Cambridge University Press, 1977);
Lord Kinross, *The Ottoman Centuries: The Rise and Fall of the Turkish Empire* (New
York: Morrow Quill, 1977).

2. With its economic potential and growing marketplace, Turkey should become the engine driving cooperation among the countries in the Black Sea region. In February 1992, the Economic Cooperation Organization, founded in 1985 by Turkey, Pakistan, and Iran, was revitalized when it accepted Azerbaijan as a new member, creating the biggest economic sphere in the Islamic world, with roughly 300 million inhabitants. On June 22, 1992, based on a Turkish initiative, the countries bordering the Black Sea founded the Black Sea Economic Cooperation instructive. In the medium term, these developments could lead to an important new market for Turkey.

3. As a member of NATO, Turkey is a cornerstone of the U.S.-led security system encompassing the Middle East and the eastern Mediterranean; Turkey draws on its ties with Israel and the Arab world. Turkey's participation in the war against Iraq for the liberation of Kuwait increased respect for Turkey in the Arab world and helped Turkey win a new and important ally, Saudi Arabia.

4. The dissolution of Yugoslavia enabled Turkey to reconsider returning to the Balkans, not as the former Ottoman imperial power but as a factor of stability and a contributor to regional peace. In 1994, Turkey sent four thousand soldiers to participate in the U.N. peacekeeping mission in the former Yugoslavia.

5. With people of Turkish origin stretching from Turkey's eastern borders toward China's Xinkiang province, Turkey may be destined to become the cultural and political role model for a whole belt of newly independent states, thus projecting its ambitions and power potential across the Central Asian landmass and even beyond the borders of China.

Turkey's potential contributions to economic, political, and security interdependence in this vast region take many shapes and forms. Turkey sees itself and is seen by others as a critical participant "in new forms of multidimensional cooperation involving Western Europe, the new democracies of Central & Eastern Europe, the new independent states emerging from the old Soviet Union and Yugoslavia and, finally, some nations of the Middle East and the Mediterranean basin."[4] It is revealing, however, that recent literature on Turkey's new geopolitics is limited with regard to Turkey's future role in Europe and its her relationship with the European Union (EU).[5]

Most studies published since 1989–90 have dealt with the subject of Turkey's relationship with the European Union in a traditional and nongeopolitical manner.[6] When "elements of politicization in the EU-Turkish relationship" have been analyzed, the perspectives have been described as "hazy."[7] The Greek-Turkish

---

4. Mehmet Ögütcü, "Religious 'Bias' in the West against Islam: Turkey as a Bridge in Between," *Dis Politika* (Foreign policy), no.18 (1994): 106; for a broader context, see Keith Krause, "Insecurity and State Formation in the Global Military Order: The Middle Eastern Case," *European Journal of International Relations* 2, no. 3 (1996): 319.

5. Graham E. Fuller and Ian O. Lesser, eds., *Turkey's New Geopolitics: From the Balkans to Western China* (Boulder, Colo.: Westview Press, 1993); this RAND study mentioned the relationship between Turkey and the EU only in passing and at the very end, without discussing the western links of Turkey as a precondition for any new and eastern-oriented Turkish geopolitics.

6. See, for instance, Mary Strang and Arlene Redmond, eds., *Turkey and the European Community* (Brussels: Forum Europe, 1992); Canan Balkir and Allan M. Williams, eds., *Turkey and Europe* (London and New York: Pinter Publishers, 1993); Mahmut Bozkurt, *Die Beziehung der Türkei zur Europäischen Union* (Frankfurt and New York: Peter Lang, 1995).

7. Heinz Kramer, "Turkey and the European Union: A Multi-Dimensional Relationship with Hazy Perspectives," in Vojtech Mastny and R. Craig Nation, eds., *Turkey between East and West: New Challenges for a Rising Regional Power* (Boulder, Colo.: Westview Press, 1996), in particular p. 215.

conflict, the Cyprus issue, the Kurdish question, and human rights in Turkey have come to the forefront but not the issue of an intensified strategic partnership with Turkey in the newly emerging "European architecture." The EU lacks a cohesive, strategic approach in its relationship with Turkey, and the same conclusion applies to Turkey's approach to Europe. "It seems highly plausible," concludes Heinz Kramer, a leading German expert on Turkey, "that in the longer run relations between the EU and Turkey will be much more influenced by developments within Europe and Turkey than by the possible strategic roles Turkey could play or be assigned in the Middle East or Central Asia."[8]

Which conclusions both sides will draw remain to be seen. Thus far, the European Union is continuing to redefine its political perspectives and its strategic choices. Turkey, and its role in the post–cold war world, has been of minor concern. Turkey, in the meantime, has been preoccupied with domestic issues, including the question of cultural identity and political orientation. Although Turkey placed its resources at the disposal of the peace process in the Balkans, it has been reluctant to explain and clarify its geopolitical view of Europe. Many members of Turkey's political and business communities have emphasized their wish to join the European Union, but Necmettin Erbakan, since July 1996 the first "Islamic" prime minister, placed his mark on Turkey's priorities by visiting Iran and Libya before any other country. He was thereupon severely criticized in Turkey, reinforcing the assessment that Turkey itself was not yet clear about its future role in the West and its relationship with Europe.

In the early 1990s the Turks were euphoric about the role their country might play in the post–cold war period; as the century closes that euphoria is being replaced with a "new realism" con-

---

8. Ibid., p. 223

cerning the potential and the possible. Turkish Islamists provoke anti-Western and anti-European feelings, which surface easily because of Europe's rejection of Turkish EU membership and its failure to protect the Bosnian Muslims. Arab countries, moreover, do not sympathize with a strong Turkey that can, for example, project power into northern Iraq, and the thought of allowing the Turks to occupy "holy Arab land" horrifies all the Arab states.

The United States, more than any other single country, continues to build its relationship with Turkey on geostrategic assumptions and projections, including expectations that Turkey will contain Iran in the East and Syria in the South, stand up against Russia in the North, and help stabilize the Balkans in the West. This same multidimensional approach helped undermine the foreign policy of the late Ottoman Empire and in fact destroy it; Kemal Ataturk, the founding father of the Turkish Republic of 1923, was well aware of the dangerous implications of such a policy. Thus in the late twentieth century, Turkey is again confronted with foreign policy problems whose resolutions will have a tremendous effect on its future role and power. Those problems are how to

1. Tame the Greek-Turkish conflict to prevent it from having a negative impact on Turkish-EU relations

2. Balance Turkish-Iranian competition, bilaterally and in regard to their respective roles in Central Asia and the Caucasus

3. Define Turkey's role in the Balkans

4. Deal with the "sick man Russia" and with the ruins of the Soviet empire

Since many nations are discovering patterns of history in order to redefine their après–cold war policies, it is not surprising that Turkey has also succumbed to that temptation. A revival of

Ottoman thinking, however, will not be sufficient to cope with the agenda of the twenty-first century. As the 1990s unravel, it is clear that Turkey is overburdened—being a pillar of stability in an ocean of troubles, on the one hand, and seeking to project its concepts of stability, cooperation, and order into all four directions of heaven, on the other hand. Turkey must, but has not yet, set priorities and focus its foreign policy agenda in order to be both cohesive and effective in pursuing it.

The hope that Turkey might play a major role in building regional order is counterbalanced by the warning that any exaggerated role for Turkey may undermine its domestic stability and, in fact, cohesion. Internal political stability indeed remains the prerequisite for any Turkish power projection. Thus far, the domestic agenda has been narrowly defined by those who are focused on the Islamic factor. Turkey's society, however, is pluralistic, and the issue of political volatility and cohesion is more important than the horror scenarios of an Iranian-type Islamic republic. Given Turkey's political culture, sound traditions, and specific religious roots, an Islamic republic is unlikely. What Turkey must face, however, are the following socioeconomic challenges, which are enormous:

- Population growth: When the Turkish Republic was founded in 1923, the population was ten million as compared with thirty million at the height of the Ottoman Empire. In 1996, the population exceeded sixty-five million.

- Uncontrolled and unlimited urbanization: Because of the large size of the country, the statistical population density is relatively low. More important is the continuous change in the rural-city relationship. In 1945, 82 percent of the population was living in rural areas and 18 percent in cities. By 1990, the ratio had changed to 60 percent in rural areas versus 40 percent in the cities.[9] One consequence is the explosion of poor areas on the periphery of all big cities (Gecekondu), with the ensuing enormous economic and social problems.

- Revitalization of the economic boom, which began with Özal's liberalization policy in 1980 and ended in severe economic crisis in April 1994: Inflation rose to 125 percent, real income decreased by one-third, the GDP rate declined 6.1 percent, foreign debt increased to US$74 million, the trade deficit reached US$14 billion, and the Turkish lira had to be devaluated by two-thirds against the deutsche mark.

- The Turkish military: What will be its role in the event of failures of political leadership such as occurred in 1960, 1971, and 1980?

- The Kurdish issue: How to develop regional growth and sociocultural integration in Turkey's Southeast.

- Finding a balance between a state-centered society and the growing forces of civil society and pluralism.

- Finding a balance between the laical foundation of the Turkish Republic and the role of the Islamic religion in public life.

As long as Turkey is undergoing the consequences of incomplete Westernization, its politics remains domestically vulnerable and handicapped in the pursuit of its foreign policy goals. Its military strength remains strong. In fact, Turkey is one of the few

---

9. See Udo Steinbach, *Die Türkei im 20. Jahrhundert. Schwieriger Partner Europas* (Bergisch-Gladbach: Gustav Lübbe, 1996), p. 339; see also Atila Eralp et al., eds., *The Political and Socioeconomic Transformation of Turkey* (Westport, Conn.: Praeger, 1993); Cigdem Balim et al., eds., *Turkey: Political, Social and Economic Challenges in the 1990s* (Leiden and New York: E. J. Brill, 1995); Ismet Ergün, "Zur Wirtschaftslage der Türkei," *Südosteuropa Miteilungen* 35, no. 4 (1995): 360.

members of NATO that has increased its military and military-industrial efforts since 1990. A new arms race is taking place in the whole region, including Greece, Iran, and Syria, for no clear reason, although there may be perceptions of insecurity in an increasingly volatile and uncertain region. The paradox is that, although direct threats to Turkish security have declined since the collapse of the Soviet Union, the risk of being drawn into confrontations has increased. Thus although Turkey's importance to regional security has grown, the country is confronted with a wave of skepticism in the West over the need to defend Turkey's territorial integrity.

The changing geopolitical landscape in Central Asia and the Caucasus is also affecting Turkey's orientation and interests. In the aftermath of the dissolution of the Soviet empire, Turkey is perceived in the West as the bridge to both the Transcaucasian republics and to the newly independent Central Asian countries. Based on Soviet census statistics of 1989, more than 49.5 million people of Turkish origin live in the countries of the Commonwealth of Independent States (CIS): around 30 million are concentrated in Central Asia, more than 10 million in the Russian Federation (around half of whom are Tartars), and almost 6 million Azerbaijani Turks live in Azerbaijan. The largest nation of ethnic Turks is Uzbekistan, with almost 17 million people; the smallest groups are the Karaim of the Crimea (3,000) and the Tofas of Siberia (800).

Turkey's economic presence in these regions is visible and relevant. The cost of Turkish construction work in Central Asia, for instance, amounts to around US$3.7 billion, exceeded only by similar work undertaken by Turkish contractors in Russia and Libya. Turkey's trade with Central Asia amounts to 16.5 percent of Turkey's total trade with all the former Soviet Union. In terms of potential prospects for cooperation, "if the Turkic states are able to extract and transport large quantities of oil and natural gas, the percentage of Turkish imports of agricultural raw materials in the commodity composition of trade would most probably be considerably reduced."[10]

The newly emerging independent states of Central Asia have also triggered cooperation between the United States, Turkey, and Israel in Uzbekistan and Turkmenistan in the field of agricultural assistance and training. As announced in October 1994, Turkey will offer its know-how on open irrigation, Israel will provide expertise in sophisticated irrigation technology, and the United States will "presumably provide finance."[11] But Turkey's ability to project its power as a regional *force d'ordre* is relative. Not only has Russia returned to the region of its direct South, in an attempt to demonstrate what the geopolitical notion of a "near abroad" could mean to a wounded, yet relevant, world power, but the Western world has begun to discover the Caucasus and Central Asia on their own terms. Instead of relying on a Turkish middleman, no matter how close he may be to Western strategic institutions, Western countries have begun to define their individual interests in the Caucasus and Central Asia. This development may imply a limited interest in these regions or it may suggest that Western countries have not yet determined how to deal strategically and economically with countries in the region, which is more likely. Turkey as a strategic force and resource in this context has been severely underrated in the West.

The foregoing does not imply that Turkey will not eventually emerge as the regional power it has been portrayed as in the search for a "new world order." It will, however, take time to recognize the substantial cultural impact of the Turkish presence in

---

10. Gareth Winrow, *Turkey in Post-Soviet Central Asia* (London: Royal Institute of International Affairs, 1995), p.38; see also for the other cited figures.

11. Ibid., p. 40; see also Werner Gumpel, "Stand und Möglichkeit einer wirtschaftlichen Zusammenarbeit der Türkei mit den Staaten Zentralasiens," *Südosteuropa Mitteilungen* 35, no. 3 (1995): 228.

Central Asia and to understand what it means. The deep cultural effects of the change of alphabet from the Cyrillic to the Latin one (with the exception of Tajikistan, which followed the Iranian recommendation and chose the Arabic alphabet) will be noticeable for generations to come. Turkey's economic performance will affect the attitudes of local partners and will continuously nurture the debate about "model Turkey" in the eastern plains and mountains. Turkey may not be able to project military power throughout the region, but Turkey has been and remains NATO's fundamental and irreplaceable partner in a region of volatility and unstable transformation. In terms of Western interests, this alone assigns a role to Turkey that is more important than that of any other country in the region.

Turkey's relevance for any Western strategy, in the near or broader region, depends on Turkey's membership in NATO. Those who seek to redefine Turkey's role in the world in terms of multiple options may do so only as long as they root their logic in the irretrievable fact that NATO membership is the single most important factor defining Turkey's standing in the Western camp. "Even as Turkey pursues new initiatives in the Black Sea and elsewhere," assesses Ian O. Lesser, "Ankara will continue to look to the United States for strategic reassurance, political support, and economic cooperation."[12] NATO membership is the basis for any Turkish strategic or operational outreach to new regions with old neighbors.

## Turkey, Germany, and Europe

The most important European partner for Turkey is Germany. Both countries are connected through a century-old relationship

---

12. Lesser, *Bridge or Barrier?* p. vi.

of cooperation and confidence. The first ambassador of the Ottoman Empire in Berlin arrived in 1783. Efforts of Sultan Selim III and Sultan Mahmut II to modernize their armies in the nineteenth century brought Prussian officers to Constantinople and paved the way for the Turkish-German alliance in World War I. Economic ties intensified during the Weimar Republic. Germany became the most important trading partner for Turkey, importing 14 percent of all Turkish imports in 1928.[13] Nazi Germany tried to prevent Turkey from joining the Allied camp, but Turkey stayed neutral, although Germany remained Turkey's most important trading partner until 1944. Turkey did, however, grant exile to leading German scientists fleeing Nazi Germany; among them was Ernst Reuter, later lord mayor of Berlin and leader of the courageous resistance against the Soviet blockade of the city in 1948/49.

The cold war brought Germany and Turkey close again, united in their quest to contain Soviet expansionism. Turkey and West Germany developed into cornerstones of the American-led Western security system and became key partners of the United States. Since the 1950s, economic ties between Turkey and West Germany have continued to strengthen. On October 31, 1961, both governments signed a treaty encouraging Turkish workers to join the West German labor market. This, the beginning of a long and prosperous history of "guest workers," represents "the human tie" between Germany and Turkey to this day.[14] That tie began with 2,500 workers. By 1996, 2.3 million Turks were living in Germany and had become "a part of Germany."[15]

---

13. Steinbach, *Die Türkei im 20.Jahrhundert*, p. 416.

14. Ayse Kadioglu, "The Human Tie: International Labor Migration," in Balkir and Williams, *Turkey and Europe*, p.140.

15. Theo Sommer, "Sie gehören zu Deutschland," *Die Zeit*, no.46 (November 8, 1996): 13; see also Udo Steinbach, "Die deutsch-türkischen Beziehungen—alte Freundschaft am Scheideweg?" *Südosteuropa Mitteilungen* 34, no. 2 (1994): 79.

In Berlin alone, 140,000 Turks have found their home—more than the number of Turks in the army of Kara Mustafa, who stood before Vienna in 1683. Most "German Turks" wish to remain in Germany and have done so, contributing to Germany's economic affluence. They pay 2.5 billion German marks into pension funds and 8.5 billion German marks in income tax. In 1975, one hundred Turks had started their own businesses in Germany; by 1996 that number had reached 41,000, with a turnover of 34 billion German marks and a capital investment of 8.3 billion German marks.

Despite these impressive facts, the Turks in Germany—whose children and grandchildren may appropriately be described as "German Turks" or "Turkic Germans"—do not enjoy all the privileges of German citizens. Like the Helots, the foreigners in ancient Greece, they cannot vote, but fourteen thousand Turks apply for German citizenship every month; yet only a handful are granted citizenship. If the rate continues at which Turks became citizens of Germany between 1977 and 1990, it will take 230 years for all Turks in Germany to be granted a German passport. During the 1990s, German authorities have become more open-minded. But based on the number of naturalizations in 1994 (2,000), it would still take 110 years to naturalize all Turks living in Germany. The issue of immigration and citizenship (or double citizenship) has become one of the most emotional topics of German political debate. Xenophobic actions against foreigners include the Turks, some of whom were killed. Although the debate about the future legal status of the Turks in Germany is not yet over, it is likely to produce a more liberal citizenship law.

In view of the large Turkish community in Germany,[16] the

---

16. Big Turkish populations in other European countries include 240,000 in France, 215,000 in the Netherlands, 150,000 in Austria, 85,000 in Belgium, 73,000 in Switzerland, 50,000 in Sweden, and 20,000 in the United Kingdom. See Faruk

Turkish-German relationship as a whole is of major importance. The experience with the Turkish population in Germany has been generally positive, and yet Germany has not fully made up its mind on the Turks and on Turkey, both with regard to the citizenship issue and with regard to Turkish EU membership. In 1963, the European Economic Community signed an association treaty with Turkey that included the prospect of full membership. Twenty-two years later, in March 1995, Turkey and the EU concluded a full customs union, which was ratified in the European Parliament in late 1995 only after heated debates on domestic developments in Turkey, notably human rights violations.

Three military coups in two decades (the most recent on September 12, 1980),[17] the military intervention in Cyprus in 1974 and the violent partition of that Eastern Mediterranean island, the practice of torture in Turkish prisons, and the protracted war with Kurdish secessionists in eastern Anatolia since the mid-1980s overshadow the political relationships between Turkey and the member states of the European Union. Even if Greece—Turkey's archenemy—did not belong to the EU, the Turkish-EU relationship would be sensitive. Whenever the debate on Turkey and its admission to the EU becomes heated—which is often—the question of compatibility between Christian Europe, no matter how secularized, and Islamic Turkey appears as well. Pragmatic solutions are difficult to find in such an atmosphere.

During the 1990s, Turkey and Europe have been emphasizing

---

Sen, "Turkish Communities in Western Europe," in Mastny and Nation, *Turkey between East and West*, p. 234.

17. The change of government in June 1997 was brought about under strong pressure by the military but came about without the evident signs of a true "military coup." In fact, the events demonstrated the strength of Turkish president Demirel and the self-correcting mechanisms of the civilian constitution, which remains under strong military supervision. For more about the June 1997 events, see the afterword on page 123.

cultural, social, and religious differences, even though the strategic relationship demands pragmatic and intensified cooperation. In 1996, the government of Prime Minister Erbakan and his Welfare Party (Refah) became the target of stern critique and sharp rejection in German and other European media because of their alleged intentions to change the laical character of the Turkish state. Although Refah gained only 21 percent of the vote and was forced to form a coalition government with the liberal-conservative and secular party of Foreign Minister Tansu Ciller, it nonetheless was labeled the first "Islamic" Turkish government. The leaders of the Turkish army, who had vested interests in the government's policies, forced Erkaban to bow to their laical demands, raising speculations about their plotting Erkaban's fall. In November 1996, when Turkish president Demirel visited Germany, he pled again for full EU membership. The German government, under strong public pressure, demanded an improved state of human rights in Turkey as a criteria for EU membership and declined to specify a timetable for membership.[18] The ensuing debates between Germany and Turkey were counterproductive and lacked a sense of perspective.

It was in 1987 that Turkey first applied for full EU membership, contrary to the advice of many of its friends inside the European Community. At that time then Prime Minister Özal was supported in his own country by an enthusiastic wave of pro-European sentiments. Frustration was therefore intense when the

---

18. See *Frankfurter Allgemeine Zeitung,* no.260 (November 7, 1996): 10; the reaction of the German government came in response to Turkish president Demirel's comment that Turkey shares the values of Europe. See also *Frankfurter Allgemeine Zeitung,* no.258 (November 5, 1996): 4. On Erbakan's foreign policy, see Faruk Sen, "Erbakan—ein Wolf im Schafspelz," *Internationale Politik* 51, no. 9 (1996): 53. In a broader context, see Atila Eralp, "Turkey and the European Community in the Changing Post-War International System," in Balkir and Williams, *Turkey and Europe,* p. 24.

European Community rejected the Turkish application in late 1989. This development coincided with the emergence of Turkey's new geopolitical outreach: it became involved in the domestic development of Azerbaijan, undertook engagements in Central Asia, and became an important pillar in the U.S.-led coalition against Saddam Hussein's Iraq. Whereas Europe rejected Turkey, the geopolitical transformation strengthened it. In 1992, Turkey launched the Black Sea Economic Cooperation instructive, held the first Turkish summit in Ankara, and recognized Bosnia-Herzegovina. Since 1994 Turkey has participated in the U.N. peacekeeping mission in Bosnia-Herzegovina to help stabilize its large Muslim population.

Still, Turkey appears to be haunted by its past. Its effort to establish itself as the leader of all "overseas Turks" (*Dis Turkler*) has been severely criticized by those in Turkish republics who do not wish to see the "elder brother" (*starshnyi brat*, the Soviet Union) replaced by an "older brother" (*agabey*, Turkey). Following the war against Iraq, Turkey was also confronted with an enormous Kurdish refugee problem, which the Turkish population helped alleviate in a most humanitarian way. The embargo against Iraq, however, ruptured important economic ties for Turkey and now poses a threat to domestic stability, as does the increasing radicalization of the Kurds in Turkey. The protracted war in Turkey's Southeast has become more and more ugly. Sympathies for the Kurds spread throughout Western Europe, to the detriment of the image of the Turkish state. In 1995, after highly emotional press coverage of the "ugly Turkish war in Kurdistan," the German government froze exports of defense equipment to Turkey. For Turkey, however, any challenge to its territorial integrity is unacceptable and therefore precludes a reasonable political solution to the Kurdish problem.

The return of Turkey to the Balkans was welcomed by the Bosnian Muslims but not universally in Europe. A new round of

Greek-Turkish verbal battles has developed, producing heated dis-
putes over the status of some Aegean islands. The two NATO partners seem once again to have difficulty choosing between enmity
and alliance. The ambivalence between Turkey's NATO role and
NATO's role for stability in the eastern Mediterranean, on the one
hand, and Turkey's relations with Europe and Europe's reserve
toward Turkey, on the other hand, is influenced and determined
by this archaic yet deeply embedded conflict of pride, jealousy,
and "open historical bills." The quarrel has been exacerbated
since Greece became a member of the EU because that membership substantially increased its weight in the seemingly eternal
debate over whether Europe should have more confidence in
Greece or in Turkey.

For Turkey, the consequences are frustrating. Although its
new geopolitical options stretch from the Balkans to western
China, its role in Europe remains elusive and undefined. What
matters are the implications. If Turkey cannot strengthen its relationship with the EU—which does not necessarily mean EU membership but implies at least the ability to participate in the procedures of the Common Foreign and Security Policy (CFSP) of the
EU and full membership in the Western European Union—it cannot successfully pursue its legitimate foreign policy goals. For Europe it would be a disaster "to lose" Turkey, but how to properly
bind it to Europe seems far from clear by mid-1997. For both
Turkey and the EU, the problem seems equivalent to squaring a
circle and remains, therefore, a major diplomatic and political
challenge that must be resolved.[19]

Both the European Union and Turkey must look for fields on
which the strategic relationship between the two can be intensified without directly touching on the issue of EU membership.

---

19. See also Metin Heper et al., eds., *Turkey and the West: Changing Political and
Cultural Identities* (London and New York: I. B. Tauris, 1993).

One approach may be to integrate Turkey fully into the WEU, the European "pillar-to-be" of NATO. Since NATO has decided that the WEU could and indeed should provide its own military institutions and matériel in NATO-approved "European" missions, Turkish membership in the WEU may be a logical consequence.

Turkey became an associate member of the WEU in 1995 and seeks full WEU membership. Although neither Norway nor Iceland belong to the EU, they both are NATO members associated with the WEU. Thus there exists other precedents. Concerning the future architecture and role of the WEU, it has been suggested that associate members should participate in future WEU missions and that the decision to undertake such missions depend on the vote of WEU members and the consent of the associate members. Greece, however, rejected the proposal. Thus, the only option left for Turkey is full WEU membership, thereby reinforcing Turkey's demand for full EU membership, provoking even more skepticism in Greece and elsewhere.[20] Yet for the defense and security pillar of the EU, full Turkish WEU membership may be another variation of how to square the circle: To accept Turkey as a WEU member would simply postpone the EU membership question. At this point in time Greece will undoubtedly seek to veto such a WEU membership for Turkey. Turkey and Greece are still both haunted by their history!

The Turkish government has continuously stressed that relations between Turkey and the EU should not be overshadowed and influenced by Turkish-Greek controversies. But escalating conflicts between the two NATO rivals are likely. Differences over the territorial shelf in the Aegean and flight paths in that region have not been resolved. Conflicting positions on the status of a microisland (Imia in Greek, Kardak in Turkish) almost produced

---

20. See Horst Bacia, "Ankaras Streben in die WEU," *Frankfurter Allgemeine Zeitung,* no. 278 (November 28,1996): 14.

a military clash in 1996 as did the dispute over military fortifications on several Greek islands. The most problematic issue of all, however, is the future of Cyprus.

Since the Turkish occupation of northern Cyprus in 1974 and the promulgation of a Turkish republic—recognized only by Ankara—Cyprus has been on the agenda of the United Nations and all Euratlantic bodies. A solution does not seem to be in sight. Until 1996, Cyprus might have been just another international diplomatic issue, watched over by U.N. peacekeeping forces, but with the application of the (Greek) Cypriotic republic for EU membership, the divided island is contributing to European divisions of opinion. Should only the Greek Cypriotic part be admitted, and should it in fact speak for the whole of Cyprus, including the Turkish North? Will Turkey fully incorporate northern Cyprus in case only southern Cyprus is admitted? Should both the Greek and the Turkish Cypriotic republics be admitted or neither of them in view of the unresolved status (and character) of the eastern Mediterranean island? In view of the intergovernmental conference that is reviewing the Maastricht Treaty of the EU in 1997, the question of a new round of EU admissions is on the table and thus so is the Cyprus question. The European Union and, for that matter, NATO must take responsibility for peacefully resolving the Cyprus issues—a resolution that cannot be left to the United Nations and international soldiers.[21]

---

21. See: Hansjörg Brey, "Zypern als Krisenherd—Konfliktpotential und Möglichkeiten der Friedenssicherung," in Wagenlehner, *Konflikte, Konfliktlösung und Friedenssicherung in Südosteuropa,* p.116; Heinz-Jürgen Axt, "Zypern—ein Beitrittskandidat der Europäischen Union," *Südosteuropa* 44, no. 5 (1995): 259; Heinz-Jürgen Axt, "Konflikttriade im östlichen Mittelmeer," *Internationale Politik* 51, no. 2 (1996): 33. From a Turkish perspective, see Hüseyin Bagci, "1996 Kibris sorununun çözüm yili olacak mi?" (Can 1996 be the year of solutions for Cyprus?), *Yeni Yüzyil* (Ankara), 1996, p. 20. From a Greek Cypriot perspective, see Werner Adam, "Klerides für eine gänzliche Entmilitarisierung. Vorschläge des Staatspräsidenten

# The United States in Europe and Turkey

With the end of the cold war, the disappearance of a clearly defined enemy has forced the transatlantic security community to
redefine its rationale. The community can only be based on two
fundamental pillars:

- The shared values, with all their implications for flexible
  and broad approaches, when taking economic, political, or
  military decisions that concern the mutual interest

- The alliance of mutually shared security and defense responsibilities that enables the community to play its key role
  as a pillar of stability and Western cohesion

Nothing is more important than defining the future role and
posture of NATO. The Dayton Agreement on Bosnia-Herzegovina
demonstrated that the Western European ability to formulate and
implement a common foreign and security policy remains weak in
the absence of American leadership. Although Europeans have
rightly complained about U.S. unilateralism on certain trade matters (the threat of sanctions against European countries that trade
with Cuba), American leadership—and for that matter a certain
amount of unilateralism—is indispensable in guiding the Atlantic
community toward a coherent and effective common foreign and
security policy.

NATO remains the most important instrument of U.S. foreign
policy, a necessary vehicle enabling the United States to play its
role as a world power. The United States, however, needs a stable,

---

der Republik Zypern an Rauf Denktasch," *Frankfurter Allgemeine Zeitung,* no.217
(September 17,1996): 3.

friendly, and cooperative countercoast in Europe. Since the Mediterranean basin is an extension of this coast, the future of its rim countries is a U.S. national security interest, as well as Turkey's. American membership in NATO is central both to the future of Turkey and to the future of U.S. involvement in Europe and the Mediterranean basin. The longer the relationship between Turkey and the European Union remains overshadowed by uncertainties, the more important the bilateral relationship is between Turkey and the United States. This relationship goes beyond defense cooperation and military ties as Turkey seeks to develop "a more diversified 'strategic relationship' featuring increased trade, investment, and defense-industrial cooperation."[22]

In purely military and defense terms, Turkey's importance cannot be underestimated.[23] Its armed forces are the second largest in NATO, with a total of 579,000 men in active service and nearly two million in reserve. Turkey remains attentive to the potential instabilities in the vast regions of the former Soviet Union, as well as those coming from the Middle East and the Arab world, especially those related to the "Kurdish struggle,"[24] led by the terrorist PKK with its bases in Iraq and Syria. Because no one has been able to resolve this question for the Turks, it is plausible that Turkey will seek to improve ties with Iran and Iraq, both of which host a large Kurdish population, to find solutions that would not affect the territorial integrity of all three host countries.

Beyond Turkey's interest in maintaining territorial integrity, it is most unlikely that it would establish strategic ties with either Iraq or Iran as an alternative to its NATO commitments. In August

---

22. Lesser, *Bridge or Barrier?* p. vii.

23. See also Dyugu B. Sezer, "Turkey's Political and Security Interests and Policies in the New Geostrategic Environment of the Expanded Middle East," Occasional Paper No.19, Henry L. Stimson Center, Washington, D.C.

24. Edgar O'Ballance, *The Kurdish Struggle 1920–94* (Houndsmills/London: Macmillan Press, 1996).

1996, Prime Minister Erbakan signed a US$20 billion agreement by which Turkey will purchase natural gas from Iran. Since December 1996, Iraqi oil has been flowing again through Turkish pipelines, following the U.N. decision to lift partially the sanctions against Iraq. To draw the conclusion, however, that such Turkish pipeline "Ostpolitik" means that "Turkey's future is in the East, not within the European Union,"[25] is superficial and is also wrong.

No matter what "Islamic" reasons may have affected Prime Minister Erbakan's decision, Turkey needs energy from her eastern neighbors to keep pace with modernization and economic development, as part of the Western strategic world. It was wise and prudent, indeed, that U.S. criticism "was limited to mild criticism from low-level officials."[26] Those who argue that Turkey belongs in the Western strategic camp must determine how Turkey can maintain and speed up its economic development *without* using natural resources from Iran or Iraq. They must also recognize that Iran and Iraq represent large potential markets for a developing Turkish export industry.

## Reemerging Cold War Debate

During the 1970s and 1980s, West Germany developed major economic ties with the former Soviet Union—including construction of gas pipelines and heavy truck plants—and was severely criticized for doing so in the United States. Critics asserted that the West Germans would gradually be pulled into the Soviet orbit. The Germans argued that, on the contrary, any substantial increase of economic and technological cooperation with the West would force the Soviet Union to open up its totalitarian structures. More-

---

25. "Get Serious about Turkey," *Wall Street Journal,* August 16, 1996, p. A9.
26. Ibid.

over, German-Soviet trade was marginal in the overall German trade balance. The political debate of the 1970s and 1980s has been handed over to the historians in the 1990s, who will now look back in order to find the objective impact of West Germany's economic Östpolitik.

An analogous political debate is taking place concerning Turkey, which is now criticized for collaborating too much with the "devils" in Teheran and Baghdad. The Turkish government argues persuasively that Turkey incurred major losses as a consequence of American containment of both Iran and Iraq during the 1990s. One can also persuasively argue, however, that this "double" containment cannot continue much longer. Indeed, it would be wise for the West to establish or strengthen economic ties with Iran and Iraq that constructively engage and incorporate the two stigmatized countries in the international marketplace, where civilized behavior governs. In the absence of a convincing and effective linkage between economic cooperation and responsible political behavior in Iran and Iraq, such an approach will remain debatable and controversial. But even the *Wall Street Journal*, critical about Erbakan's "Ostpolitik," has concluded that Western strategy should "reaffirm its commitment to a Western-oriented Turkey."[27]

One factor in this context is the oil and gas potential of the Caspian Sea region. Strategically, it may appear to be of secondary importance to the direct power equation between Turkey, Russia, Iran, Iraq, and the United States. But the oil poker game in the Caspian Sea region may affect that equation.[28] The International Energy Agency predicts a decrease in the Organization for Economic Cooperation and Development's crude oil share in the

---

27. Ibid.
28. Curt Gasteyger, "Ölpoker am Kaspischen Meer," *Frankfurter Allgemeine Zeitung*, no. 106 (May 7, 1996): 12.

world market from 24 percent in 1991 to 15 percent in 2010; the Organization of Petroleum Exporting Countries' share is predicted to increase from 30 to 48 percent. The Middle East will remain the most important exporter of oil to the West, while production of North Sea oil will decline. In this context, the future of the oil (and gas) resources of the Caspian Sea area becomes important, if only to balance direct dependency on Middle East oil.

At one time the Caspian Sea had only two rim countries—the Soviet Union and Iran. Today, however, it is considered the sea of five countries: Russia, Iran, Turkmenistan, Kazakhstan, and Azerbaijan. According to Western estimates, Kazakhstan, richest in resources among the Caspian Sea countries, will increase its crude oil production from 26 million tons in 1992 to 67 million tons in 2010. The Tengiz field at the northwestern corner of the Caspian Sea is considered to be the biggest unexplored oil field in the world, containing 1.5 to 2 billion tons of crude oil. Kazakhstan's gas production will increase from 8 billion cubic meters in 1992 to 25 billion cubic meters in 2010, mainly from the Karachaganak fields. In 1991, Turkmenistan contributed 105 billion cubic meters to the gas production of the Soviet Union and today seeks to intensify production with the help of Western investment, looking even to the huge Chinese and the Indian markets.

Azerbaijan, the oldest oil-producing country in the world, suffered a decrease in its production of crude oil during the 1980s but has become the most advanced oil player among the Commonwealth of Independent States (CIS) in recent years. In September 1994 an international oil contract was signed in Baku with Azerbaijan's state oil company, which has a 20 percent interest. British Petroleum has a 17 percent interest, and four U.S. corporations together hold 40 percent; in addition, a Russian company (Lukoil) holds 10 percent, Norway's Statoil holds about 8 percent, and Turkish Petroleum has been involved since September 1996 with a share of 5 percent. Turkey's role in this "Azerbaijan international oil consortium," however, is larger than shares in the contract indicate because Turkey controls the Bosporus Straits and thus will help determine how oil pipelines will carry Caspian Sea oil to its markets in the West.

The Azerbaijan International Oil Consortium has selected two routes, one connecting Baku with Noworossijsk in Russia (via Chechnya) and the other running between Baku and Batumi in Georgia. There is also the prospect of a direct pipeline from the Caspian oil fields either through Turkey (ending at the Mediterranean port of Ceyhan) or through Iran (ending at the Persian Gulf). It should be evident where U.S. interests lie.

The most cost-efficient route leads from Baku via Armenia into Turkey, but the politics of memory and power might prevent it. The Turkish genocide against the Armenian people during the last years of the Ottoman Empire has never been forgotten by the Armenians, even though Armenian leaders played a role as well. Armenians as victims of a genocide can rely on strong sympathy in the United States and in Europe, particularly in France, with its large Armenian exile population, but Armenia does not have strong connections with other Western governments. Thus despite its independence, Armenia continues to remain dependent on Russia, including the Russian military. The Nagorno-Karabach conflict ended in a stalemate between Armenia and Azerbaijan that left Azeri territory occupied by the Armenian army, producing new tensions between Armenia and Turkey. The common border has been closed at Turkish initiative, to the detriment of Turkish merchants in northeastern Turkey. Diplomatic relations between the two countries remain frozen. The Armenians complain that Turkey prevents their nation, the oldest Christian nation on earth, from joining Europe. Armenia, seeking to join the Council of Europe, sees its way to Strasbourg blocked by Ankara, a route that Azerbaijan also seeks to follow.

The Transcaucasian conflicts are nurtured by the emergence

of old and new rivalries following the collapse of the Soviet Union and reflect to a great extent the continuous efforts of Russia to maintain its influence using a policy of divide and rule. The world's media look at Chechnya, but other countries can tell their own stories (e.g., conflict in the Georgian secessionist region Abchasia). The relationship between Armenia and Azerbaijan, like overall development in the Transcaucasian republics, is not only of interest to the Commonwealth of Independent States but affects Turkey's role as a regional power and the interests of the West in all three Transcaucasian republics. Although the European Union has not presented a clear definition of its interests in the Transcaucasus, the United States should act differently concerning the Caspian oil "game" and the relationship between Turkey and Armenia. The Transcaucasian and Caspian regions may appear to be of marginal importance, but they are critical to the future equation of power among Turkey, Russia, Iran, and the West.

For Turkey, "it can exert its influence only within and through an international system."[29] A stable, strong, and democratic Turkey is in the interest of the West and of Turkey, if it is to play a respected and leading role as a regional power. As to the triangle of Turkey, Germany, and the United States, the following should be kept in mind:

1. The West needs a strong Turkish partner, not only in bilateral terms, but as a key player in Western political and strategic architecture. In this regard, NATO provides the strongest anchor, making Turkey a cornerstone of security and stability on NATO's southern flank.

---

29. Andrew Mango, "Turkey: The Challenge of a New Role," Washington Papers No. 163, Westport/London, 1994, p. 121.

2. The United States perceives Turkey primarily as a strategic asset, whereas the European states tend to concentrate more on conditions in Turkey, in particular human rights and problems of democratic consolidation but also on the divide between Christianity and Islam. These two different approaches produce different conclusions concerning how firmly Turkey should be anchored in Western institutions as a whole. The United States favors more intensive integration with Europe, but the European Union is not prepared, at this point, to accept Turkey as a member.

3. For Turkey, membership in NATO can provide an effective security system, creating the necessary basis on which to develop its political and economic interests in the East. This assertion has been convincingly proven with regard to NATO. Turkish membership in NATO is hence to be considered reliable and sound and remains in the interests of Turkey and the alliance as a whole.

4. Concerning Turkish relations with the European Union, attitudes are ambivalent and the situation unresolved. Whether the European Union will fully incorporate Turkey will remain an open question for years to come. It can and should not be excluded provided the Turkish record on human rights and economic progress becomes convincing and provided the EU will have properly developed sound means and mechanisms of "flexible integration," leaving room for multifaceted membership schemes. At present EU membership for Turkey appears to be permanently postponed; membership in the WEU may, however, occur but remains a topic of dispute in Europe. If the EU continues to respond to Turkish interest in membership with simple postponement tactics, it will surely produce the

very frustrations the EU seeks to avoid. By contrast, the EU does not wish to be pressed on this matter by the United States, which will not help the Turkish cause by blaming the EU for not doing enough to anchor Turkey in Europe.

5. The alternative, to be either a regional power or part of a vague and undefined European architecture, is artificial and unacceptable. As long as Turkey is not accepted as a full member of the European Union, Western-oriented Turkey will see this as the rejection of a century of self-imposed Westernization. Such growing frustrations could, in the worst of cases, lead one day to radical rejection of its European partners, to the detriment of its Atlantic ties. None of the countries in the equation of Turkey–EU–United States is interested in such a negative development.

6. The most realistic approach would be to anchor Turkey firmly and continuously in the Atlantic security system (NATO) and gradually bring it into European political and foreign policy structures (CFSP and WEU). Such an approach will provide Turkey with the foundation and stability with which to act as a regional power in its own interest and in the interest of the West as a whole. This approach requires more attention and greater flexibility from both NATO and the EU, as well as from the United States and Germany as Turkey's most important partners in the West. There is no realistic alternative to the triangle of Turkey, Germany, and the United States.

Turkey today has new choices and new options, which it will only make constructively as a firmly committed member of the West. Germany is in a strong position to help Turkey, the EU, and the United States. But Germany can do so only if its approach is balanced, which presupposes that Germany makes up its own mind on the role Turkey is to play in Europe. The United States has renewed its commitment as part and partner of the architecture of European security, but in the triangle of the United States, Germany, and Turkey, it is the Germans and Turks who must lead.

## Afterword

In June 1997 Turkey's first pro-Islamic prime minister, Erbakan, resigned "under heavy pressure from a military leadership that . . . declared him and his constituency a danger to the nation's secular tradition."[30] The long-term significance is clear. Turkey will continue its struggle between two worlds: the world of democracy and that of Islamic fundamentalism. "The generals," writes Stephen Kinzer, "believe that by forcing Mr. Erbakan from office, they have crushed a grave threat to Turkish freedom. To them, Islamic political power means obscurantism, fanaticism and ultimately dictatorship. Others see it as simply a response to what growing numbers of Turks want."[31]

Who or what will prevail is another question, as is how this struggle will affect Turkey's relationship with what the country's military considers to be the Western civilization of Kant and Tocqueville.

---

30. Kelly Couturier, "Turkey's Islamist Premier Resigns," *San Francisco Chronicle,* June 19, 1997.

31. Stephen Kinzer, "Islam and Liberty: Struggles in 2 Lands," *New York Times,* June 22, 1997.

*Henry S. Rowen*

CHAPTER FIVE

# The Uncertain Future of the Atlantic Alliance

The American commitment to Europe's security after 1948 had two main purposes: foremost, protecting Western Europe from the Soviet Union and, second, fostering a strong, democratic Europe that centered on bringing Germany into the European community of nations. Both have been accomplished.

Although an expansionist Russia might return, lowering the odds of that happening should be a cardinal aim of Western policy. Western Europe has long since relinquished America as a guarantor of its internal cohesion and prosperity. Although the future always contains surprises, those who worry that Germany will again attempt to dominate Europe underrate the profound changes in that country. The largest concern that Americans should have about the future of Europe is not a revival of German militarism but Europe's incapacity to act coherently on security matters.

That there are many shared interests between Europeans and Americans is not in doubt. The main questions are (1) What security challenges are Europe and America likely to face in the coming decades and how can they best be handled? (2) Can and should the North Atlantic Treaty Organization (NATO) survive in its present form? and (3) What, if anything, are the Europeans going to do about building a serious security institution?

Considerations bearing on these questions are the following:

- Western Europe has become a zone of peace within which conflict has become extremely unlikely.

- There is now no immediate, serious threat to Europe or the United States—other than nuclear weapons in Russia and China.

- New dangers will emerge, possibly from Russia and certainly from some developing countries, especially those in the Islamic belt to Europe's south and southeast.

- The future character of Russian politics is uncertain. A democratic polity in that country is the best way to assure Europe's security.

- Nuclear weapons, along with chemical and biological ones, pose the most serious threats. Nuclear threats might come from loss of government control of readily fissionable material in Russian stocks or from independent development by other countries.

In the twentieth century both the United States and Europe have been much better off when the United States has been engaged with European security than when it has not. There is no good reason to doubt the validity of this proposition as the twenty-first century approaches. However, this leaves open the suitability of arrangements that were made during the cold war.

# The Past

Although the United States had become the world's leading economic power by the beginning of the twentieth century, it refused to be deeply engaged politically and militarily with most of the world, until it was attacked in 1941. After World War II the view prevailed that the war might have been averted had we stayed involved with Europe after World War I and that the Great Depression might not have been so great had we taken the lead in maintaining the international financial system. These beliefs, together with the challenge from the Soviet Union, led the United States after 1945 to play the leading role around the world in security, trade, and finance.

In Europe, it was evident that a prostrate region would need large amounts of economic aid, that the Soviet Union was implacably hostile, and that a transatlantic alliance was needed. That alliance was also seen as insurance against any German militaristic resurgence. After the attack on South Korea in 1950 (encouraged by Stalin), a large military buildup seemed necessary. There was no alternative to the United States taking the lead in all of this, initially financing much of it.

During the cold war it was said that NATO served three purposes: "keeping the Americans in, the Russians out, and the Germans down." With time, however, it became evident that the Germans did not need to be "kept down"; instead they became thoroughly democratic and among the most ardent of Europeans. Not only have former national animosities been overcome, but much progress has been made toward creating a federation of European states. However, the other two purposes remained vital until the end of the Soviet empire.

Despite much rhetoric over the years about the alliance having "two pillars," the Western European Union (WEU), which was created for that purpose, never acquired much authority, in part because a serious WEU was seen as incompatible with a serious NATO. The perceived essentiality of NATO in sustaining and winning the long competition with the Soviet Union, together with uncertainties about the future, makes its members unwilling to let go. But the transformation of Germany and the disappearance of the task of keeping the Russians out, at least for the near future, raises the question as to why the Americans should be "kept in"? The stock answer is reassurance against possible future dangers. Two of these have been identified: an expansionist Russia and places conventionally identified as "out of area." Although the first of these dangers cannot plausibly be represented as imminent, something could happen regarding the second at any time. The 1990s have seen two major events under this heading: the 1990–91 gulf war and the crisis in the former Yugoslavia. More are likely.

## The Atlantic Nations in a Transformed World

There are two contrasting views of the environment in which the Atlantic nations will live.

### AN INCREASINGLY DEMOCRATIC
### BUT STILL TURBULENT WORLD

The world is undergoing rapid and fundamental change. Most dramatic has been the disappearance of the Soviet Union, but much more is under way. At bottom is a worldwide movement away from collectivism toward market capitalism. In East Asia, the move of China from communism to capitalism is taking place more slowly, but that transition may turn out to be the most important world development of the latter part of the twentieth century. The shift is also well under way in South Asia and Latin America. As a

result, there has been a large improvement in economic performance among countries that have given the most scope to markets, including Argentina, India, the Czech Republic, Hungary,
and Poland. Russia has also made radical economic changes, but
its economic output is still depressed by dislocations produced by
trying to transform an overindustrialized command economy into
a market one and by internal conditions that discourage new investment.

Only two large regions have lagged: the band of Islamic countries from North Africa through the Middle East (highly salient
for the West) and West and Central Asia. Per capita incomes in
North Africa and the Middle East have dropped by 2 percent a
year since 1986. The other lagging region is sub-Saharan Africa.

This process of economic liberalization will produce a gradual
convergence of incomes in the developing countries with those of
the industrial ones. That convergence is well under way in much
of East Asia and will occur more widely. This implies that the share
of world economic output produced by today's industrial countries (most of whom are members of NATO, with Japan the main
exception) will fall from about 60 percent in 1990 to about 40
percent in 2020.

That convergence implies a slow decline in the power of the
Atlantic states, but many other factors—of which the most important is that many authoritarian or unstable democratic countries
will become stable democracies, a projection based on the fact
that all high-income countries have become (more or less) democratic—will be at work. The transition to stable democracy begins
at a per capita gross domestic product (GDP) of between $5,000
and $6,000 (in 1995 purchasing power parity dollars) and "be-
comes impregnable" at $7,000.[1] (High incomes from removing

---

1. Adam Przeworski, Michael Alvarez, Jose Antonio Cheibub, and Fernando
Limongi, "What Makes Democracies Endure?" *Journal of Democracy* 7, no. 1 (1996).

raw materials, notably oil, from the earth do not produce this effect.) Growing incomes are accompanied by increased education, the building of civic institutions, and the formation of attitudes that enable democratic governments to survive when they have a chance at power. Spain, Portugal, Chile, Argentina, Taiwan, and South Korea all made the democratic transition at this income range.

Looking ahead, chances are good that Russia will reach the $7,000 threshold within a decade. Growth of China's per capita GDP, if sustained, will bring it to that level by around 2015. Consistent with this pattern, the North Central European countries are becoming solidly democratic. The outlook for South Central Europe, including the Balkans, is less promising, given its ethnic divisions and the slow progress of economic reform.

Two other phenomena are crucial in understanding the likely future international environment: One is that most democracies are clustered geographically in regions that are peaceful (e.g., North America, Western Europe, and, increasingly, South America), whereas authoritarian ones are in regions marked by political turmoil and conflict.[2] The projected increase in democracies should result in the growth of existing peaceful areas, as well as new ones. The other is that democracies tend not to war with one another; thus the future environment might be more benign.

Of greatest direct importance for Europe and the United States, in addition to Russia, however, are the Muslim countries of North Africa and the Middle East because of their proximity to Europe and because most of the world's low-cost oil is in the Middle East. (Also of enormous importance, especially to the United States, is the future political character of China.)

The prospects are not good for the Islamic belt. None of its

---

2. Max Singer and Aaron Wildavsky, *The Real World Order* (Chatham, N.J.: Chatham House, 1996).

governments has embraced the liberalism essential for good economic growth, and all have current or latent political instabilities. In Turkey, which is important because of its size, location, Western orientation, and NATO membership, Islamic radicalism is on the rise, its politics are unstable, its economy mismanaged, and it has failed to address adequately the claims of its Kurdish citizens. (Many Turks believe that Islam is the reason Turkey is not being admitted to the European Union.) A conflict between Turkey and Greece—both NATO members—would violate the norm that democracies do not fight.

## HUNTINGTON'S VIEW THAT CIVILIZATIONS WILL CLASH

A very different vision of the future has been advanced by Samuel Huntington, who asserts that future international alignments—and conflicts—will be along "civilizational" lines.[3] In his lexicon, the existing civilizations, largely formed along religious lines, are Western, Eastern Orthodox, Islamic, Confucian, and so forth. He sees the West as declining in influence, Islam as exploding demographically with destabilizing consequences, and non-Western civilizations as reaffirming their values. The West's universalist pretensions increasingly bring it into conflict with Islam and China. "Fault-line" wars, largely between Muslims and non-Muslims, generate "kin-country" rallying and threats of escalation. The survival of the West depends on Americans reaffirming their Western identity and Westerners preserving their civilization against challenges from others.

Economic growth is altering the balance of power between Asia and the West, specifically the United States, making non-Western cultures and values more attractive, as witness Turkey, Singa-

---

3. Samuel Huntington, *The Clash of Civilizations and the Remaking of World Order* (New York: Simon and Schuster, 1996).

pore, and Pakistan. A wide revival of Islamic ideas, practices, and rhetoric has resulted in conflicts with non-Muslim societies. Thus, the early years of the twenty-first century are likely to see the clash of peoples of non-Western civilizations with the West and with one another.

In Huntington's view, in the emerging world, no country has global security interests and global power is obsolete. A political Europe, centered on Germany and France, is being created whose historical boundaries are those of Western Christendom. Its eastern boundary separated Western Christianity from Orthodox Christianity and Islam. The countries to its west should become members of the European Union and NATO, whereas those to its east should cleave to the Orthodox or Islamic civilizations. (Turkey and Greece are anomalies, Turkey because, although Islamic, is a member of NATO, and Greece because it is an Orthodox outsider in Western institutions whose memberships will become more tenuous and difficult.) Russia should be responsible for order within its Orthodox population and along its borders. Ukraine, divided between Western Christendom and Orthodoxy, might break up but is more likely to cooperate with Russia. Russia and the West might work out an accommodation that would include Western acceptance of Russian primacy for maintaining security among Orthodox countries and a favorable attitude toward Russia's difficulties with its Muslim peoples. The most violent fault lines at the local level are between Islam and its Orthodox, Hindu, African, and Christian neighbors. The fourteen hundred years of conflict between Islam and Christianity, both Western and Orthodox, will continue. Overall, the dominant division is between "the West and the rest," with the most intense conflicts between Muslim and Asian societies on the one hand and the West on the other. The most dangerous clashes are likely to arise out of Western arrogance, Islamic intolerance, and Sinic assertiveness.

Global economic development will diffuse military capabilities. Japan, China, and other Asian countries will become more powerful, as will Islamic societies and Russia if it reforms its economy. Acquiring weapons of mass destruction is seen as countering the West's advantage in conventional arms and appeals to states that aspire to be regionally dominant. They can also threaten the West directly. Efforts to stop this process will fail.

The central challenge for the United States is reversing its moral decline and recognizing the common culture that unites Europe and America. Whether the West comes together politically and economically depends on the United States reaffirming its identity as the leader of Western civilization. Western elites need to rethink policies left over from the cold war including guarding against a resurrected Soviet Union.

Although the disagreement between these two visions is not total, it is large. Huntington denies the reality of the multiplicity of identities people have—the family, tribe, nation, and sect—and focuses largely on religion.[4] Moreover, modernization is modifying many of these identities; hostility to the West is in part hostility to the effects of modernization. Particularly striking is the extent to which countries within given civilizations have *not* rallied to their brethren in trouble: Islamic countries in the gulf war were aligned on both sides, and in Bosnia civilizational alignments have been muted and mixed up (France and Britain, pro-Serb; Germany pro-Croat; and the United States, weakly pro-Bosnian). Many interests and alignments cut across civilizations, and most conflicts—Hutus versus Tutsis, Pathoons versus Tajiks, radical Algerian Islamists versus less radical ones, Kurds versus other Muslims—do not and probably will not occur along civilizational lines. Some, however, are "intercivilizational": Serbs versus Croats or each of them versus Bosnian Muslims. Nonetheless, both visions

---

4. Pierre Hassner, "Morally Objectionable, Politically Dangerous," *National Interest*, winter 1996/97.

agree on the growing increase in the economic and military power of non-Western countries.

## External Dangers Facing Europe and America

Two sources of actual or potential threat to Europe have been identified: from Russia and from so-called out-of-area directions. This distinction derives from the perception that an attack by the Red Army was long seen as the overriding, indeed for Europeans the only, threat to Europe. With NATO a defensive alliance, the conviction developed that it could only act "in area," and not counter hostile Soviet actions elsewhere. After the mid-1960s, the probability of the Red Army attacking Europe diminished sharply, but the Soviet Union stepped up its activities elsewhere, supplying arms and advisers to Vietnam, Libya, Egypt, Syria, Algeria, and India, with extensive involvements in East and southern Africa (much of it via the Cubans), and invading Afghanistan. The task of countering these actions was left largely to the United States, with Britain, France, and others occasionally taking action.

### THE RUSSIAN THREAT

Russia does not pose an invasion threat today to Western Europe or even to the countries of Central Europe. The present incapacity of the Russian military needs little elaboration, witness its incompetence in Chechnya. Indeed that institution's poor condition should be a cause for concern to the West because a disaffected military might contribute to internal developments that could become dangerous to outsiders.

The greatest immediate threat from Russia lies in its many nuclear weapons combined with its unstable politics. Some of these weapons are on long-range missiles and could quickly be launched. Conceivably, some could be launched by people in lower levels of authority, but the more dangerous possibility is the loss—or sale—of portable tactical weapons or stocks of fissionable materials to terrorists or states such as Iran looking for a short-cut way to get nuclear weapons.

The Russians have engaged in campaigns of subversion, coercion, and threats against members of the former empire and may be supporting terrorists against Turkey via Armenia and the Kurds. Its activities against the near abroad countries do not directly threaten the West but are an ominous indicator of future problems. This behavior fuels the worry that Russia might acquire a regime that tries to recreate some approximation to the Russian empire, a development that would be threatening to Central Europe and elsewhere. It has caused the Central Europeans to clamor for NATO membership and is a principal reason why the NATO members have agreed to admit three of them.

OUT-OF-AREA THREATS

According to Michael Mandelbaum, "There is no compelling reason to believe that turbulence on the periphery of the international system will affect its center."[5] This is an unwarrantedly optimistic view of the dangers to the West from certain kinds of developments, including "turbulence" on the periphery.

The single greatest danger is from nuclear weapons and other mass-destruction weapons used against the forces or territories of the West. Also of concern is the growing ability of potentially hostile nations to acquire advanced conventional weapons that might limit the ability of Western countries to act out of area in defense of their interests.

Two recent conflicts have damaged or threatened these inter-

---

5. Michael Mandelbaum, *The Dawn of Peace in Europe* (New York: The 20th Century Fund Press, 1996), p 39.

ests: that in former Yugoslavia from 1991 and the 1990–91 gulf war. Aggression—and genocide—in Europe were not only evils in themselves, but the West failed to stop them despite its ability to do so. That was not only demoralizing but a bad signal to send to those who might be contemplating making trouble (such as Saddam Hussein and Iran's leaders). As for the gulf war, not only did it threaten the world's main source of oil, but it was carried out by a country well advanced in acquiring weapons of mass destruction.

Moreover, some states, notably Iran, Iraq, Syria, and Libya, support terrorism both against one another and also against the West. Iran and Iraq are known to have nuclear weapon programs; these and others have chemical and biological warfare programs and also ballistic and cruise missiles. We may be on the receiving end of them some day.

## Does Europe Still Need American Protection?

A distinguished historian has written that "even with the disappearance of the Soviet threat, the American presence remains an intrinsic part of the European security system. . . . Russia remains a power, and a nuclear power, on a scale that still requires American strength to balance if Europe is not to militarize itself to a degree inconceivable even at the height of the Cold War. Further, the reunification of Germany, however benign the policy of its leaders, has created a new, or rather re-created an old, power-center on the continent that makes the states of Eastern as well as Western Europe (and not excluding those of the former Soviet Union) anxious to retain the US as part of the regional balance. The disappearance of American power would leave Europe from the Atlantic to the Urals prey to terrifying uncertainties. . . . For Central and Eastern Europe it would be a real disaster."[6]

6. Michael Howard, *Survival* 36 (1994).

That opinion is shared widely in Europe, but there are difficulties. First, it was one thing for the United States to commit to, and spend heavily on, European defense to combat an evil empire whose forces were in the center of Europe; it is another to commit to allaying European uncertainties—at least without examining how realistic they are. Second, our presence creates an incentive for the Europeans to do less. This has always been true, but now the common danger is less clear. Third, the forces and money that we allocate to Europe might hurt our ability to deal with challenges elsewhere. In any case, if America is to continue to help defend Europe, to what end and how should its power be deployed?

Given the history of the past century, the possibility of trouble emanating from within Europe cannot simply be dismissed. Fears were widely expressed at the time of German unification that Germany would become the most powerful European state and that it would gain hegemony—at least economic—over Central and Eastern Europe. Even though Germany is a model democracy, some people question how it might use this strength. As the distinguished scholar of nationalism, Elie Kedurie, put it:

> As an historian who has to consider the past, which is the only evidence he has, I must warn against mistaking the present peaceable pictures for the whole of reality. . . . Mass enthusiasms can grip any population . . . there can and should be a balance of power between states, because that is our only fully tested safeguard against international disorder."[7]

Although that observation arguably understates the transformation that has occurred in German values and self-identity, an-

---

7. Elie Kedurie and George Urban, "What's Wrong with 'Nationalism,' What's Right with the 'Balance of Power'? A Conversation," in U. Ra'anan et al., *State and Nation in Multi-Ethnic Societies: The Break-up of Multinational States* (Manchester, Eng.: Manchester University Press, 1991), pp 238–39.

other reason not to be concerned is that Germany will not have a hegemonic position within Europe. Although its national output is greater than that of any other single state in the union, it constitutes only 30 percent of the total and lacks dominance in military technologies. The probability of a militaristic Germany that needs to be "balanced" against is small indeed. Although some hold this position to be "bold, if not foolhardy," to fix one's gaze on the past is to risk miss looming dangers—and opportunities.[8]

There are other possible sources of instability in Europe. Much attention is now focused on assuring the stability of Central Europe and keeping it from being (again) a field of contention between East and West (about which more below). There could be wider trouble in the Balkans, and too little attention is being paid to Turkey.

On the face of it, Europe should be able to take care of itself. It faces few immediate threats, is far richer than potential adversaries, is technically as advanced as any region, and has come far in economic and political unification. Much turns on its future political character. The union has been both "widening" and "deepening," two processes in tension. The widening—the incorporation of Austria, Finland, and Sweden—has brought in successful and stable countries. But more members multiply interests and make collective decisions more difficult. The deepening process furthers integration but not for all of them, at least not all at the same rate. This is displayed in the two-tier movement toward a common currency.

The union has gone far in the economic dimension, but the Maastricht Treaty goes much further politically, for example, in creating a common European currency. Much of this remains

---

8. Timothy Garten Ash, "Germany's Choice," *Foreign Affairs,* July/August 1994, p. 67.

highly controversial; for instance, the French were divided down the middle on Maastricht, *and* it is not clear that the Germans will give up the deutsche mark for the Eurodollar. But whatever the prospects for Maastricht, the least developed of Europe's institutions are those for foreign policy and defense. Economics aside, the Europeans have become highly inward looking. A French analyst writes that the most severe obstacle to the transatlantic alliance may be the inward-looking tendencies of the Europeans rather than the neoisolationist ones of the Americans.[9]

There have been several reasons for European underdevelopment on foreign and defense matters: The United States has often been willing to act, especially on out-of-area challenges. Another is the aforementioned differences in their security perceptions. Also, there is no natural leader; although Germany's economy gives it the capacity to play that role, it is not accepted as such nor has it sought it. So, often by default, the United States has taken the lead largely through a superior capacity to act based on greater unity of purpose and more resources. When it has not led, as in former Yugoslavia, the results have usually been unfortunate. Now the (at least apparent) absence of threats lowers the Europeans' incentive to do anything serious about collective defense. It also renders changes in the American connection to Europe less risky.

A crucial weakness of Europe is that Russia will remain a strong nuclear power and that there is no West European counterpart force or a credible one in the offing. It is doubtful that French and British nuclear weapons would be an adequate counterweight, despite French suggestions that it could shield Germany against a Russian threat. The Europeans need a robust counter to Russian nuclear strength, and there is no currently feasible alternative to the United States' providing it.

---

9. Dominique Moïsi, *Financial Times*, November 15, 1996.

## The Uncertain Character of Russia

The Central Europeans want protection against the possibility of a revived, hegemonic Russia. Although the recent large steps toward democracy in Russia are welcome, they also see nondemocratic forces and behavior that look all too much like the past. For economic, security, and cultural reasons they want to be fully part the West.

To West Europeans, the prospect of a resurgent Russia is also worrying, although perhaps less than to a Central European, given the eastward movement of Russia's military power. Nonetheless, Russia has the potential in the long run to have Europe's largest national economy and to be its greatest military power.

Much turns on future Russian politics. There are both unfavorable and favorable aspects from its past—including its recent past—to contemplate. Russia has been a centralized, authoritarian society through its history and was never part of the Roman Empire. "We never had feudalism, the more's the pity," Pushkin said. The philosopher Berdyayev wrote that "there was no Renaissance among us." Sergei Witte, the modernizing finance minister in the late nineteenth century, wrote in 1905: "Russia in one respect represents an exception to all the countries of the world . . . the exception consists in this, that the people have been brought up over two generations without a sense of property and legality."[10] Richard Pipes observes that orthodoxy became virtually a national religion, one that resisted the secularization that occurred in Western Europe, and that the notion of private property was alien, with the crown treating all property as its own until the end of the eighteenth century and in some ways long after that. This status

---

10. Richard Layard and John Parker, *The Coming Russian Boom* (New York: Free Press, 1996), p. 24.

of property was related to the absence of representative bodies and to the weakness of the rule of law. There were independent courts only from 1864; the courts never pronounced on constitutional matters, and there were no suits by private citizens against the government. Serfdom inculcated in the peasants contempt for law and property and a resistance to all authority because there were no responsibilities and benefits of citizenship. Because the system rested on force, the regime had to prove its might through territorial acquisition; in so doing it became a great power. When that status progressively declined through defeat in wars, so did the reputation of the monarchy. In Russia, the sense of identity was always linked to empire and its loss has produced bewilderment and anguish. Moreover, such rule of law as existed under the tsars was destroyed under the Communists. Although the recent progress toward democracy is impressive, the Communists won the largest number of seats to parliament in the 1995 election and nondemocratic parties won nearly half of the seats. Moreover, Russia's politics are unstable.[11]

Russia's foreign behavior today should be deeply worrying. It has been interfering in the internal affairs of several neighbors in the near abroad, notably, Moldova, Georgia, Tajikistan, and Azerbaijan. This interference has had several aims, varying by country, but, overall, it results in Russia having military bases and forces in many of the countries to its south and considerable influence over them. Russian claims that these are defensive moves lack plausibility.

Russian intervention in Georgia, for example, has been extensive: "All of Georgia's minority problems have been exacerbated by Russian interference."[12] In Abkhazia, a Georgian province that

---

11. Richard Pipes, "Russia's Past, Russia's Future," *Commentary*, June 1996.
12. Paul Henze, "Russia and the Caucasus," *Studies in Conflict and Terrorism* 19 (1996): 389–402.

had a small Abkhaz population relative to the Georgian one, Russian arms, encouragement, and sponsored mercenaries drove the Georgians and many others out. Although Russia has come to recognize recently that a stable Georgia is in its interest, Abkhazia remains in ruins.

In Azerbaijan, the election of 1992 brought into power an independent-minded Ebulfez Elchibey; Moscow then supported a coup against him. His successor, Heidar Aliev, a former member of the Soviet politburo, turned out to be as independent minded—and has been the target of many allegedly Russian-supported plots.

The story in Chechnya is similar insofar as it has involved Russian aggression but different in that Chechnya is a part of Russia and the remarkable brutality of the Russians. The results to date (with the longer-term outcome unclear) are thousands of deaths from indiscriminate and incompetent military operations, the destruction of Grozny, the defeat and demoralization of the Russian military, and a loss of popularity for Yeltsin.

Paul Henze notes that "even Russia's democratic leaders argue that Moscow has the right to intervene in the Near Abroad." Moscow, however, has been unwilling or unable to control the actions of military and security officials in these new countries, but those actions are inconsistent with the professed desire of elected officials to have a democracy, to respect human rights, and to be respected and supported by the West. More such behavior will produce condemnation by the West (which should have more strongly by now). This is not a "Monroe Doctrine" case. That was about keeping European powers *out;* this is about the *insertion* of Russian power. Russia needs to abandon its neocolonial mentality.[13]

Henry Kissinger's view is stark. He sees the Russians as pro-

---

13. Ibid.

grammed to engage in imperial drives even though both the tsarist and communist empires collapsed, materially and spiritually exhausted by overextension. They will exploit any gray zone allowed to exist between Germany and Russia in Central Europe. Continued ambivalence by NATO toward strengthening the Atlantic alliance and toward Russia will tempt an even further expansion of Russia's frontiers.[14] To Kissinger, the evidence is clear: Russia is reembarked on an imperialist path, and the West needs vigorously to counter this threat.

These substantial views notwithstanding, there is another side to the case. There are positive elements in Russian history: Most of Russian literature, music, and art has been Western in character, and for three centuries it has insisted on being regarded as European. Recently, there have been relatively honest elections, and nongovernment institutions are being created at a great rate. For example, there has been a virtual explosion in the number of independent, voluntary organizations since the abolition of the Communist Party's monopoly of power. (A recent listing of those organizations required ten volumes.)

Today, decrees and laws passed by the Moscow government are widely ignored throughout the country. Richard Pipes sees the situation as similar to that after February 1917, with the important differences that the country is not at war and that utopian fantasies are missing. The present government is the first in its history to have a popular mandate to build a viable democratic system. The problem is the political inexperience of the Russian people. The sense of isolation survives along with suspicions of the West, suspicions heightened by the proposed expansion of NATO.

Much of life for the Russian people today is dominated by dislocations with declines in incomes (although official figures exaggerate its extent) and the loss of job security. Another is the

---

14. Henry A. Kissinger, "Beware: A Threat Abroad," *Newsweek,* June 17, 1996.

shock of losing the empire after centuries of expansion. Nevertheless, a poll taken in April 1996 shows that, although two-thirds of
Russians have the image of Russia as a country whose "greatness
from the past must be extended into the future," no more than
one-fifth want to see the Soviet Union restored; less than one-
tenth are willing to make some sacrifices to restore it; and only
one-third support Russia reuniting with republics having signifi-
cant Russian populations.[15] Only 10 percent say that they support
using force to that end. Thirty-three percent of Russians endorse
the total separation of Ukraine from Russia. Although 61 percent
see "the US as using Russia's current weakness to reduce it to a
second rate power and producer of raw materials," and 85 percent
would like to have full "military parity with the US," large majorities favor cooperation with the West and have favorable opinions
of the United States. No more than 10 percent support radical
nationalism.

Although these views are encouraging, such opinions, whatever their current accuracy, may not be good predictors. As Elie
Kedurie said, "Mass enthusiasms can grip any population." As Vladimir Shlapentokh puts it, intellectuals and politicians are found
in three groups: liberals, moderate nationalists, and radical nationalists. The liberals want a Western-type of democracy, the radical nationalists want an approximation to the Russian empire
under authoritarian rule, and the moderate nationalists (for
whom Alexandr Lebed might become their leader) have some
yearning for a great Russia but see the reality of a weak Russian
economy, a lack of order, crime and corruption, and demoralization of the army and people. They support cooperation with the
West for instrumental reasons, in order to recover. They see time

---

15. Vladimir Shlapentokh, "How Russians See Themselves Now: In the Aftermath of the Defeat in Chechnya," unpublished paper, Michigan State University,
December 1996.

as needed before they can achieve reunification with the other two Slav states, Belorus and Ukraine.

Much depends on the economy, which might have reached bottom in 1996 and now has a good prospect for growth. Richard Layard and John Parker point to the extensive liberalization of the economy and the high educational level of the work force as supporting their estimate that growth over the next decade should be 4–5 percent annually. From today's depressed level of output (perhaps $5,000 per capita gross domestic product [GDP] in international prices), and assuming that 1997 marked the bottom of the transition from a command to a market economy, this implies a per capita GDP of $7,000–$8,000 in about a decade, the level for attaining a stable democracy.

Layard and Parker see the main obstacles as the weakness of the rule of law and the associated phenomenon of powerful mafias, which discourage foreign investors who, on the favorable basics of the economy, would otherwise be investing on a large scale. Even here there is hope because the new owners of property, however it was acquired, have an interest in preserving their stake through the rule of law. Moreover, extensive privatization has raised a formidable obstacle to the return of communism. In the view of Layard and Parker, the Russians will muddle along under a regime of pseudodemocracy and quasi-capitalism. To Pipes, the worst of the realistic scenarios is the model of Pinochet's Chile; were such a regime to come to power, it would likely be succeeded by a democratic one.

As for anything like the old empire being reconstituted, the most important country is Ukraine. The division between its Russianized east and non-Russianized west is an ethnic fault line that could be exploited by Moscow. Much depends on how successful the government in Kiev is in creating a better life for the people and in building a stronger Ukrainian national identity. Initial blunders in economic policy and the continuing resistance to rational policies by the parliament suggest that Ukraine might not survive a determined Russian effort to divide it and bring it back under some form of control by Moscow. The power of nationalism should not be underestimated, however, and such an attempt by Moscow would probably cause it a lot of trouble.

Belorus, a country with a weak national identity, is the best bet for reincorporation. Because that would move the Russian border back to Poland, such an event would cause alarm there and elsewhere. Another candidate for a change in borders is Kazakhstan, which has a large Russian population in its north; an effort to bring all of Kazakhstan back seems unlikely because not many Russians want more Muslims in their country. As for other parts of the former empire, the Baltic peoples and those of the Caucasus, who have long fought Russian domination, would resist losing their independence—with the Caucasians better positioned to sustain armed resistance but with the Baltic peoples better able to draw on political support from the West.

In short, if border changes occur, the most likely would bring back territory with high concentrations of Russians, but any overall reconstruction of an empire whose resources would be controlled by Moscow is unlikely. Moscow's influence within near abroad countries will be large but not equivalent to "controlling" them, especially in getting their peoples to fight wars on Russia's behalf. Today, Moscow faces a considerable task in gaining control even over all of Russia.

What about its military potential? Although Russia has about half of the population of the former Soviet Union, a capitalist Russian economy will be much more productive than was a communist Soviet Union. It has a large nuclear establishment, and its technical-military institutions, although much reduced and demoralized, can be revived. It has the basis for rebuilding a strong, conventional military force.

Assuming an average growth at 4 percent annually from 1996,

Russian per capita GDP in 2020 would be about $13,000 and its total GDP around $2,000 billion. By comparison, the United States, the countries making up today's European Union, and China are each likely by then to have national outputs of around $10,000 billion (Japan's will probably be around $6,000 billion). The aggregate output of the members of NATO will be about $20,000 billion (with Germany alone at about $2,500 billion, about the same as Russia). In short, even with respectable growth, Russia's economy will still be much smaller than most of these others. Although military power is only imperfectly correlated with economic size, the way to bet is that the country—or a coherent alliance—with many more resources will win a conflict.

Russia faces south and east as well as west. Although serious trouble seems unlikely to come from the south (Russian claims to the contrary notwithstanding), the Far East is another matter. Immediately after the Soviet breakup the idea was circulating that the Maritime provinces might split off. The region is rich in resources, and many of its inhabitants seem to find rule by distant Moscow onerous; however, they have today much de facto autonomy, and the topic of independence has receded. More serious is the growing power of China. Although Russia and China have decent relations today, China has long regarded part of Russia's Far East as having been lost to it via "unequal treaties." Its Russian population is small, and it has several million Chinese trying to earn a living. A powerful China might try to rectify its perceived historical losses, especially if Russia were to fall into internal disarray or become preoccupied externally.

What, then, to conclude about Russia? It should be regarded as a work in progress, one that might be influenced from the outside. The best assurance for a secure Central (and Western) Europe is for Russia to become stably democratic—implying the adoption of Western norms. A Russian regime bent on re-creating the empire and throwing its weight around is most unlikely to have a liberal, open, and productive economic system. Although a return to communism is ruled out, a return to a highly controlled, regulated—and poorly performing—economy is not. Further aggressive behavior internally and in the near abroad is a crucial indicator. If it continues, Kissinger's dire view will turn out to have been warranted.

## "Out-of-Area" Missions?

Troubles have come to Western Europe and North America from zones of instability and conflict, notably, North Africa, the Middle East, and the Balkans, according to the following categories:

- Military attacks on Western forces or territories (e.g., on American and other naval vessels)

- Terrorism, including taking of hostages (by several Islamic countries and groups)

- Genocide, "ethnic cleansing," civil conflicts, and other large-scale violations of human rights, which, among other evils, produces refugees (former Yugoslavia, Algeria)

- Denial of oil supplies (the tanker war with Iran and Iraq's invasion of Kuwait)

- Denial of freedom of the seas (Persian Gulf, Qadaffi's closing the Bay of Sidra)

The alliance has resisted acting on such dangers because any given event (e.g., a terrorist attack) usually affects only one or a few members at a time; the perceived interests diverge (Bosnia); the offense is not grave enough to warrant taking action (as with most threats to Persian Gulf oil); an inhibition against acting outside borders (Germany); military action seems inappropriate (most causes of refugee flight); or the expectation that the United States will handle the problem (many instances).

Among future missions that have been mentioned, one is peacekeeping, an activity that has been dubbed "social work," perhaps suitable for the United Nations but not for NATO. However, a more robust task, peace enforcing, might be another matter. That is what NATO's role in Bosnia ought to be about, but the rules of its engagement have been too restrictive. The tergiversations of Western leaders together with the weak mandate when they finally acted should make one pessimistic about NATO peace enforcing.

An obvious way in which Western countries could again become embroiled out of area includes coping with yet another threat to the oil of the Persian Gulf. Possibilities include invasions, domestic upheavals, and attacks on shipping. Military forces of Western countries seeking to secure access to Middle East oil could be the target of advanced conventional weapons (bought in the West or Russia) or mass-destruction weapons (perhaps developed with help from Russian technologists, North Korea, or China, along with components from the West). Another way in which Western countries might be embroiled is through efforts to control terrorism emanating from this area—possibly on a larger scale than so far has occurred.

TECHNOLOGY AND WEAPON FLOWS

The importance of having superior military technologies and tactics has been repeatedly demonstrated, not only in the gulf war but also, for instance, in the Korean War, in Israel's battles against the Arabs, and, by Britain, in the Falklands/Malvinas war. Superior technology did not prevent an American defeat in Vietnam, a French one in Algeria, or a Soviet one in Afghanistan, so better technology sometimes is not sufficient; but the advantages of having superior capacities to sense, process, and communicate information and to hit targets are enormous.

These capabilities are migrating from today's advanced countries to less advanced ones, some of which will strive to become major military powers including Russia, China, and India. Russia already possesses many technological strengths, and China, South Korea, India, and others will advance in them because they are integral to modern economies. The industrialized countries, who invent almost all military technologies, will continue to have an advantage as long as they continue to invest strongly in them. Moreover, as Israel has repeatedly demonstrated and as Iraq in 1991 illustrated, in a negative way, at least as important is the ability to develop the doctrines, tactics, and skills to use them effectively, and it is not clear how long this will take.

Iraq's oil wealth enabled it to increase its military spending vastly from the mid-1970s while increasing civil consumption and building many civil works. It trained many technologists, who built a large military-industrial complex. It created capacities to develop nuclear weapons and to assemble and make ballistic missiles and chemical and biological warfare agents. Iraq also illustrates limitations to this process. After many years of conflict it managed to gain an advantage over Iran, but when up against first-rate opposition in 1990–91, its organizations, human skills, and tactics were woefully inadequate. Had Iraq taken more time to improve the skills of its armed forces and had it faced a less formidable adversary than the coalition, these military investments would have made a better showing. In particular, if it had operational nuclear forces, there is a question about the willingness of the coalition to have taken it on.

Many relevant technologies are becoming increasingly difficult to control. Technologies are available to anyone that makes the required investments (including social ones). Technology flows—including those for weapons—among countries have become of great importance. Trade is one path. In the past, the West and the Soviet Union were the main suppliers, and, as the number of technically competent countries grows, it has become difficult to control this flow. Russia has a large array of offerings, North Korea is a major supplier of ballistic missiles, and China is in this market. Iran has just received a third submarine from Russia. Overlaps between technologies provide a civilian cover for foreign purchases of materials used in weapons. Therefore governments interested in getting weapons without advertising the fact label their activities "peaceful," intended for civilian purposes.[16] Another path is the transfer of humans skills, arguably an even more important one than the transfer of materials. An example is A. Q. Khan, a Pakistani engineer who worked for URENCO, the centrifuge enrichment company in the Netherlands, who returned to create the Pakistani centrifuge program for its nuclear weapon program.

WEAPONS CAPABLE OF MASS DESTRUCTION

Perhaps the single-most striking fact about the role of nuclear weapons since their introduction to the world fifty-two years ago is how few countries able to make them have done so. The ratio of the number of countries that *possess* nuclear weapons to the number *able* to do so shows a marked decline over time. Moreover, until recently the possessors of nuclear weapons have been relatively prudent and competent states. (Russia and Pakistan look decidedly less so today.)

The reluctance of countries to obtain these weapons is shown by the following:

---

16. Albert Wohlstetter et al., *Swords from Plowshares* (Chicago: University of Chicago Press, 1977).

- Any of the developed countries could have acquired these weapons long ago; only four have done so (United States, United Kingdom, France, Israel).

- A score or more economically less advanced (but in the Soviet case technically advanced) countries have had the capacity to develop nuclear weapons, but only five have done so (Soviet Union, China, India, Pakistan, and South Africa). This makes a total of nine nations having *developed* these weapons. With the nuclear weapons legacy from the former Soviet Union to Russia, Belorus, Ukraine, and Kazakhstan, there became twelve states *possessing* nuclear weapons in 1992. With South Africa's becoming nonnuclear and Kazakhstan, Ukraine, and Belorus returning their weapons to Russia, there are now apparently eight nuclear powers.

The large majority of nations capable of having these weapons have elected not to have them for several reasons:

- Weak perceptions of threat, perhaps because they are in a peaceful zone and confidence is buttressed by a collective security system.

- The absence of hostile designs on other nations.

- Incorporation in a political system that prohibited it (notably the Soviet empire) or discouraged it (the Western one).

- Domestic opposition on prudential or moral grounds, including worries about who would control them including distrust of future regimes. (South Africa's decision to dismantle its weapons was probably motivated mainly by coming political changes.)

- Expected hostile reactions from other nations.

Most of the fifty to seventy nuclear-capable but abstaining countries, including advanced ones such as Germany, Italy, Switzerland, Sweden, and Canada, are in relatively peaceful regions. Argentina and Brazil, both of which have dropped their nascent nuclear weapon programs, are also in a relatively benign environment. Most countries in zones of instability, however, including the vast area from the Maghreb through the Middle East to Central and South Asia and beyond, were technically and socially unable to carry out such complex technical programs.

It is fortunate that key aspects of nuclear weapons remain somewhat difficult to acquire fifty years into the nuclear age. Although there are no nuclear secrets left to the assiduous student, it requires some technical-industrial organization, competent people, high-quality materials, and time to develop and build deliverable weapons. Obtaining readily fissionable material remains a nontrivial task for not-very-competent governments. However, it is axiomatic that the ability to accomplish any given technological task becomes easier from the date of its introduction. Formerly exotic materials or processes become less exotic, cheaper, and more widely used in commercial products. A nuclear weapons program is now a medium-cost, medium-technology one.[17] General economic development may not be necessary; some nations with low per capita gross national products (GNPs), such as India and China, have many competent technologists, and they first tested nuclear explosives when their per capita GNPs were abysmally low. Neither Pakistan nor Iraq is an industrial power.

Unfortunately, chemical and biological weapons are cheap. That potent nerve agents are easy to make is shown by the fact that a Japanese sect made and used them. Apparently, there are several chemical programs in the developing world, especially in

---

17. Michael May, "Nuclear Weapons Supply and Demand," *American Scientist,* November–December 1990

North Africa and the Middle East. As for biological agents, the potential set is vast and generalizations are dangerous, but clearly small quantities of some of them, appropriately delivered, can cause large numbers of deaths and be difficult to defend against. Moreover, the rapid pace of bioengineering is opening up a potential for new ones. Biological agents can also present severe problems of controllability to the user, problems that are mitigated when the targets are cities many hundreds of kilometers away—as were Tel Aviv and Riyadh during the gulf war (fortunately without their use on that occasion).

The magnitude of the barriers to be overcome by a less developed country in such a program depends on its aspirations. It might be content, at least for some years, with having only few warheads and a few aircraft or ballistic missiles such as the Scud. Such a program might be seen as adequate to deter or coerce weak neighbors or to deter intervention by more powerful advanced countries. India's program resulted in a test in 1973 (labeled "peaceful" but signaling that India was a nuclear power of sorts) but was not vigorously pursued thereafter for many years. The small Pakistani program is seen as an essential deterrent against a militarily superior India. However, some countries might see the need for a robust effort. The production complex might be the object of attack, as has happened twice to Iraq, and Pakistan has also obviously worried about an attack on its facilities by India. Weapons and associated facilities have to be guarded, and they need protection from attack through dispersal or location underground. Especially if they are to be integrated in military operations, there must be command, control, communications, and intelligence systems. All this adds to costs.

Any state could move these weapons to practically anywhere on earth. (In the novel *The Fifth Horseman* Qaddafi sent a nuclear bomb into New York harbor in a ocean freighter.)[18] Anyone with a long-range civil aircraft has the means of delivering a bomb over great distances. Of particular worry is the prospect that nations like Iraq, Iran, or North Korea will be able to deliver nuclear, chemical, or biological warheads with cruise or ballistic missiles. Cruise missiles of several-hundred-kilometers range (hard to detect and intercept) are becoming ubiquitous and can be launched from land, aircraft, and ships. If one's ballistic missiles are able to travel several hundred kilometers, as does the Scud, not much more energy is required to send them several thousand kilometers (although developing the technologies for multiple stages and reentry can take many years). For instance, the Israeli Jericho medium-range missile with additional stages has put a satellite in orbit. The Chinese-made CSS-2 missiles in Saudi Arabia are capable of reaching Western Europe, and there have been reports of Saudi Arabia seeking nuclear warheads for them. In short, the ability to deliver weapons longer distances is inexorably increasing, and although Europe is closer to some possible launch sites than is the United States, the difference in exposure, if any, will not last long.

This variety of delivery means should serve as a caution to those who believe that the answer to this class of threats is ballistic missile defenses, either for military forces in the field or for national territories. These might turn out to be cost-effective against the threats for which they are designed, but there are many for which they are not designed, notably attack by cruise missiles.

How might the drastic changes the world is now experiencing alter motivations for having these weapons? Heightening the demand is the fact that the perceived threats have not only not di-

---

18. Larry Collins and Dominic Lapierre, *The Fifth Horseman: A Novel* (New York: Simon and Schuster, 1980).

minished for everyone, but they have increased for some. For instance, Pakistan's loss of support from the United States has spurred its bomb and missile programs. All the countries apparently trying to get nuclear weapons are in unstable zones. The problem of "loose nukes" in Russia has been mentioned. Coups, revolutions, and factional fighting could result in the loss of control or the use of such weapons. At some point governments or domestic factions that engage in terrorism against the West could have powerful weapons available. Any assumption that they will not be used is not justified; Iraq has used chemical agents against Iran and against its Kurdish population.

## The Uncertain Future of NATO

Mandelbaum writes that out-of-area missions are desirable but not feasible because Western publics will not support them, whereas NATO expansion is feasible but not desirable.[19] As for his first assertion, the American public has repeatedly supported such missions (most recently in Bosnia) and so have the British and the French.

Although there is more warrant for his second assertion, the commitment to NATO expansion is now past the point of return. It would have been better if the European Union had led with its expansion to the east rather than NATO, but that was not to be. The union has deferred bringing in any Central Europeans, perhaps until well after 2000. Its political energies are focused on deepening, especially creating a common currency. More important are powerful interests (especially labor and farmers) that do not want competition, along with high unemployment rates, mak-

---

19. Mandelbaum, *Dawn of Peace*, p. 46.

ing governments unwilling to push the issue. Because this unemployment is structural, not cyclical, it will persist, and opposition to bringing the Central Europeans in will continue. This is a serious strategic error because bringing them into the union would be an effective way to "Westernize" them without inducing Russian hostility. Mandelbaum puts it pungently: "In the post-Cold War era it seemed politically easier for Western governments to agree to risk nuclear annihilation in order to protect Hungary's borders, for example, than to allow their own citizens to buy Hungarian tomatoes."[20]

NATO expansion was proposed by the United States in 1994 at a time when the Europeans had just agreed to the Partnership for Peace initiative (one with little content so far) with Russia and other countries in the east. Since then, it has, without enthusiasm, been endorsed by the European members. Even the Germans, who might be thought most positive about having "Western" neighbors and a protective glacis between them and Russia, have not been of one mind.[21]

The Russians seem unimpressed by the argument that expansion helps protect them against the Germans. Instead, it dramatizes their loss of standing and feeds the xenophobia that is a prominent feature of their politics. There is no pressure now from jingoist public opinion to reconstitute the Soviet Union, but the elite might have its own aspirations and lack of popular support might not be enough to stop it.[22] The Russians claim that they have the right to an equal say on security issues in Europe; indeed they are seeking veto power over NATO decisions. They are pressing for the nondeployment of foreign troops in Central Europe

---

20. Ibid., p. 50.
21. Ash, *Germany's Choice*.
22. Stephen Sestanovitch, "Geotherapy: Russia's Neuroses and Ours," *National Interest*, no. 45 (fall 1996).

and no building of military infrastructure there. They say that they will not sign an agreement for cooperation with NATO that excludes such obligations, and without such an agreement the Duma will not ratify Start II because it would weaken Russia's ability to defend itself against an approaching military alliance.[23] It has also given the Russians an argument for reincorporating Belorus into Russia because it is needed for their defense.

The extension proposal also makes it clear who is excluded from membership, notably the Baltic states and Ukraine. The Baltics are excluded because inclusion was deemed too much of a slap at Moscow together with their indefensibility, which can be construed as writing them off. Finland's prime minister, Paavo Lipponen, has said that Europe could be divided into new spheres of interest.[24] "That is why I am asking the Americans if they realize they are riding not a tiger but a bear," he said. "Do they really know what they are doing? Is this NATO enlargement really well thought out? I still don't get what the real goal is." Finland and Sweden are afraid that an explicit decision regarding the Baltic states will destabilize the area either by provoking Russia or by compromising their independence. They prefer to foster regional security through broad cooperation, from trade to joint crime fighting, rather than military alliances. Lipponen ruled out a security zone led by Helsinki and Stockholm and supports the Baltics joining the EU. Alexandr Lebed has made a similar proposal, calling for a pan-European security system to deal with nuclear terrorism, organized crime, and natural disasters.

There are other prices to be paid for NATO expansion. The Partnership for Peace agreement might turn out to be costly. Pro-

---

23. Aleksei K. Pushkov, "The Risk of Losing Russia," *New York Times,* January 21, 1997.

24. *Financial Times,* September 17, 1996.

posed earlier, it became overshadowed by expansion, and now, in an effort to assuage Russian objections, it is being reemphasized. Former Secretary of Defense Perry has said that Russia could be involved in *virtually everything the alliance does* except the fulfillment of Article 5 ("The parties agree that an armed attack against one or more of them in Europe or North America shall be considered an attack against them all," emphasis added). This formula would enable Russia to participate in many NATO meetings and forums for military planning. For instance, U.S. officials have suggested that Russia post officers to the International Military Staff.[25] There is reluctance within the NATO military establishment to bringing in Central European officers who long served in the Warsaw Pact; to invite possible future adversaries in will produce a still less candid process. The likely result is a multiple-tier military structure.

So wide-ranging are these U.S. proposals that some NATO members, and would-be members, fear that the alliance's ability to carry out its core functions could be watered down. The United States has already said that NATO has no intention, plan, or reason to put nuclear weapons in the east, and it is unlikely that U.S. or German forces will be stationed there. One view is that Article 5 should be deleted altogether, or at least not applied to its new members, on the grounds that the United States will otherwise be called on to defend every contested frontier in feud-prone Central, Eastern, and Balkan Europe; that the United States would overextend itself much too far to the east; that America would undertake to go to war to defend distant countries that, while we wish them well, are not vital to our interests; or that guarantees would be given that in a crisis the country would refuse to honor. NATO should become a more normal regional organization.[26] Indeed, something like this last seems inevitable, as an apparent

---

25. In Norway in October 1996, *Financial Times*, October 3, 1996.
26. David Fromkin, *New York Times*, December 18, 1996.

absence of threats together with the desire to placate the Russians will make it a weaker organization.

What about the other extreme? Should NATO include Russia on the grounds that a wider policy of inclusion makes more sense than one of exclusion. This might seem fanciful for an alliance founded to "keep Russians out," but Secretary Perry's statement quoted above goes almost that far. The argument is that Russia is now a democratic, market economy with no serious differences with the West and with many common interests, including dealing with coming challenges from the turbulent, largely Islamic south. If membership in NATO is positive for democratic politics, as claimed at the time for Germany, Spain, Portugal, and now for the Central Europeans, it might be for Russia as well. Besides, when it recovers it will have political and military assets useful out of area.

The negatives are obvious and large. Suspicions of the Russians are strong, and participation would, to say the least, hurt cooperation within NATO. Moreover, unless a line were to be drawn within Russia, say, the traditional boundary of Europe at the Urals, such incorporation would take NATO territory to the Pacific and make NATO territory contiguous with that of China, a nexus that should give any prudent person pause. Moreover, continuation of the kind of behavior demonstrated by Russia in Chechnya and the near abroad is sufficient to rule out this option. The Russians say that they want to be regarded as Europeans, but this implies behaving in a more civilized way both at home and abroad.

Adam Garfinkle says that the key issue is not how large NATO should be but what the U.S. role should be.[27] It might be thought strange for the United States to be playing such a large role in Europe's defense now, for when the North Atlantic Treaty was

---

27. Adam Garfinkle, "NATO Enlargement: What's the Rush," *National Interest,* winter 1996/97.

signed in 1949, a permanent American garrison was not contemplated and Congress was told that it was not anticipated. That presence is held to be needed now because the Europeans do not trust themselves and because they do not want to handle Russia on their own (with Russia's nuclear arsenal being the most legitimate worry). Also, insofar as they think about threats from the south, they see the Americans as playing an essential role in coping with them. On balance, at least until Russia's politics stabilize, to reduce the American presence very much more would invite too much risk for what might be gained.

Another cost to NATO expansion, a topic that has displaced attention to other and potentially more serious contingencies, is that the likelihood of serious trouble seems greater elsewhere in Europe (other parts of the Balkans, Greece versus Turkey) and other out-of-area places than with Russia.

## Conclusions

"It is axiomatic that the security of America and Europe are linked."[28] In the end, not many people are willing to bet that one of the most painful lessons of the twentieth century—that the peace of Europe depended on the presence of the Americans— does not apply to the twenty-first century. That said, the Europeans would be prudent to pay more attention to strengthening their own defense institutions because if NATO comes to have no serious purpose it will become ossified and eventually lose American public support—although some kind of Atlantic alliance is likely to survive.

The consequence of NATO expansion is not clear. The Rus-

---

28. Zbigniew Brzezinski, "A Plan for Europe," *Foreign Affairs*, January/February 1995.

sians are trying to reduce its content while promoting their own role. We need to make the Russians understand that they will affect the process less through their diplomatic maneuvering and more through how they treat their own peoples and the near abroad countries. The worse they behave, the more content will go into expansion and the less into their role in the Partnership for Peace.

The West Europeans need to keep being pressed on expanding the union. If they keep temporizing, the question of why Americans should be put at risk because they cannot face dealing with Hungarian tomatoes might become a major political one.

Finally, serious troubles are more likely to come from the zone of turbulence to Europe's south than from any other quarter. We need to work harder collectively on these dangers.

# CONTRIBUTORS

DENNIS L. BARK is a senior fellow at the Hoover Institution. He holds a Ph.D. degree from the Freie Universitaet Berlin. His work includes a two-volume history of the Federal Republic of Germany, written with David Gress, now in a second edition—a history that was described in the *New York Review of Books* as "a work of impressive scholarship, comprehensive scope, and narrative power, which will doubtless be the standard history in English for years to come."

ROBERT CONQUEST, the author of *The Great Terror, The Harvest of Sorrow*, and many other books on Russian and international affairs, is a senior research fellow at the Hoover Institution.

LUDGER KÜHNHARDT was a professor of political science at Freiburg University from 1991 to 1997, where he has also acted as dean of the Philosophische Fakultaet. Currently he is the director of the Centre for European Integration Research and University Professor at the University of Bonn. He has served as a speechwriter for former German president Richard von Weizaecker and has held visiting research positions in Europe and the United States. Among his publications is his most recent work, published in 1996, *Beyond Divisions: Essays on Democracy, the Germans, and Europe.*

DOMINIQUE MOÏSI is deputy director of the Institut Francais des Relations Internationales in Paris, editor in chief of *Politique Etrangere,* professor at the Institut d'Etudes Politiques de Paris, and a contributing columnist for the *Financial Times* of London. Moïsi is also a founding member (1996) of the Club of Three, bringing together leading policymakers, industrialists, and bankers from France, Germany, and the United Kingdom.

HENRY S. ROWEN is a senior fellow of the Hoover Institution and a senior fellow of the Institute of International Studies, Stanford University. An emeritus professor of Stanford's Graduate School of Business, he has been president of the RAND Corporation and assistant secretary of defense for international affairs.

# INDEX